THE MODERN MILLIONAIRE MATRIX

Blueprint for 21st Century Wealth

Shah Rukh

CONTENTS

INTRODUCTION

In the ever-evolving landscape of the 21st century, the concept of wealth has taken on a new dimension, transcending traditional paradigms and expanding into uncharted territories. As we open the pages of this book, we embark on an exploration of the dynamic interplay between modernity, innovation, and the pursuit of wealth, guided by a blueprint that is redefining the path to prosperity.

"The Modern Millionaire Matrix: Blueprint for 21st Century Wealth" is a journey into the heart of contemporary wealth creation, where the conventional roadmaps are being rewritten and new possibilities are emerging. In this digital age, the formula for success is no longer confined to static principles; it is an ever-evolving matrix that requires adaptability, foresight, and a mastery of both the traditional and the innovative.

Gone are the days when wealth was measured solely by financial abundance. In our interconnected world, wealth encompasses not only monetary gains but also knowledge, networks, technology, and the ability to create meaningful impact. This book is an exploration of the intricate threads that weave together the modern millionaire's success story—a story that is as much about entrepreneurial thinking and leveraging the digital landscape as it is about embracing innovation and fostering sustainable growth.

As we dive into the chapters that follow, we will traverse the diverse landscapes of the 21st century wealth matrix. From understanding the mindset shift from scarcity to abundance, to harnessing the power of disruptive technologies, navigating the digital landscape, and capitalizing on emerging investment opportunities, each chapter is a portal to unlocking a facet of the modern millionaire's journey.

The blueprint we uncover in this book is not a one-size-fits-all formula but a versatile guide that empowers you to create your unique path to wealth. It invites you to embrace the opportunities presented by the digital revolution, harness the power of data and innovation, and navigate the complexities of the global marketplace. It encourages you to transcend boundaries, cultivate social capital, and harness the potential of the gig economy.

"The Modern Millionaire Matrix: Blueprint for 21st Century Wealth" is your compass in the dynamic seas of modern prosperity. It invites you to adapt, innovate, and leverage the tools and insights that define the contemporary landscape. As you read these pages, you'll gain not only a deeper understanding of the modern millionaire's mindset but also a practical roadmap that equips you to navigate the ever-changing currents of wealth creation.

So, fasten your seatbelt and prepare to embark on a journey that fuses the wisdom of traditional financial principles with the boundless potential of the digital age. The pages ahead are your guide, your mentor, and your catalyst for transformation. As we explore the depths of the modern millionaire matrix, may you be inspired, informed, and empowered to embark on a path of wealth creation that resonates with the spirit of the 21st century—a path that leads not only to financial prosperity but also to a legacy of innovation, impact, and meaningful success.

CHAPTER 1: INTRODUCTION: DECODING THE MODERN MILLIONAIRE MATRIX

Introduction: In an era marked by rapid technological advancements, globalization, and unprecedented access to information, the concept of wealth generation has taken on a multifaceted and intricate form. The term "Modern Millionaire Matrix" encapsulates the intricate network of strategies, mindsets, and opportunities that contemporary individuals navigate in their pursuit of financial abundance. This paradigm shift in wealth creation has been fueled by the convergence of digital platforms, new economic models, and changing social dynamics, all of which have collectively redefined what it means to be a millionaire in the 21st century.

The Evolution of Wealth: From Traditional to Modern: To appreciate the complexity of the Modern Millionaire Matrix, it's essential to first acknowledge the historical trajectory of wealth creation. Traditionally, wealth was often tied to physical assets, land ownership, and industrial ventures. However, the advent of the digital age has ushered in a paradigm shift, where intangible assets such as intellectual property, online platforms, and data-driven insights have gained prominence. The Modern Millionaire Matrix represents a departure from the linear accumulation of wealth to a dynamic and interconnected web of strategies that leverage technology, innovation, and human capital.

Diverse Pathways to Modern Millionhood: Within the Modern Millionaire Matrix, there exists a diverse array of pathways through which individuals can attain millionaire status. These pathways encompass various sectors and industries, including technology, finance, entertainment, entrepreneurship, and more. The rise of tech moguls, social media influencers, fintech disruptors, and e-commerce entrepreneurs exemplifies the diverse routes that can lead to substantial wealth accumulation. Consequently, the matrix defies traditional notions of a singular path to success, emphasizing instead the need for adaptability and an entrepreneurial mindset.

Technological Catalysts and Disruption: Central to the Modern Millionaire Matrix is the role of technology as a catalytic force. The proliferation of the internet, the advent of mobile devices, and the rise of artificial intelligence have not only democratized access to information but have also revolutionized business models. E-commerce platforms, for instance, have enabled individuals to reach global markets from the comfort of their homes, blurring geographical boundaries and creating unprecedented opportunities for wealth generation. Similarly, the gig economy and remote work culture have redefined labor dynamics, allowing individuals to monetize their skills on a global scale.

The Psychology of Wealth in the Matrix: Navigating the Modern Millionaire Matrix requires more than just a strategic understanding of technological trends. It demands a nuanced understanding of the psychology of wealth. The mindset of the modern millionaire encompasses traits such as risk-taking, resilience, adaptability, and a growth-oriented perspective. Embracing failure as a learning opportunity, fostering a strong sense of self-belief, and maintaining a long-term vision are hallmarks of individuals who successfully traverse the matrix. Additionally, the matrix challenges traditional notions of materialism, emphasizing the importance of purpose-driven wealth that aligns with personal values and societal impact.

The Matrix's Societal and Ethical Implications: As the Modern Millionaire Matrix continues to evolve, it raises important societal and ethical considerations. The concentration of wealth in the hands of a few tech giants, the potential displacement of traditional industries by automation, and the digital divide between different segments of society all pose critical challenges. Ethical wealth creation within the matrix involves responsible resource allocation, diversity and inclusion, and a commitment to addressing the broader societal impact of one's endeavors.

Conclusion: Navigating the Ever-Evolving Matrix: In conclusion, the Modern Millionaire Matrix represents a paradigm shift in the way individuals approach wealth generation. It encapsulates the intricate interplay between technology, innovation, psychology, and societal dynamics in the 21st century. The matrix underscores the importance of agility, adaptability, and a growth-oriented mindset in navigating the multifaceted pathways to financial success. As the matrix continues to evolve, those who decode its complexities while upholding ethical principles will be poised to not only achieve personal prosperity but also contribute positively to the broader global landscape.

CHAPTER 2: REDEFINING WEALTH IN THE 21ST CENTURY

Introduction: The 21st century has brought about a profound reevaluation of the concept of wealth. No longer confined to the traditional notion of mere financial abundance, wealth in this era encompasses a multifaceted array of elements that extend beyond material possessions. As society grapples with evolving values, changing technology, and increasing interconnectedness, the definition of wealth has expanded to include factors such as well-being, knowledge, social capital, and environmental sustainability. This paradigm shift reflects a deeper understanding of the intricate interplay between personal, social, and global prosperity.

Beyond Financial Capital: The New Components of Wealth: In the modern context, wealth transcends the accumulation of financial capital alone. Instead, it comprises a constellation of components that collectively contribute to a more holistic sense of abundance. These components include:

1. **Human Capital:** The skills, knowledge, and expertise possessed by individuals have become crucial assets in the 21st century. Continuous learning, adaptability, and innovation are now key drivers of wealth. As automation and artificial intelligence reshape industries, the ability to acquire new skills and stay relevant in a rapidly changing job market is a form of wealth.

2. **Social Capital:** The relationships and networks individuals cultivate play a significant role in defining their wealth. Collaborative partnerships, social support systems, and community engagement contribute to a sense of belonging and well-being. In the digital age,

social media and online communities also serve as platforms for building and leveraging social capital.

3. **Health and Well-being:** Physical and mental health are invaluable aspects of modern wealth. As awareness of well-being's impact on productivity, happiness, and overall quality of life grows, individuals prioritize activities and practices that promote physical fitness, mental resilience, and emotional balance.

4. **Time and Freedom:** The ability to manage one's time and enjoy personal freedom is a form of wealth that has gained significance. Flexible work arrangements, remote work options, and advancements in productivity tools enable individuals to balance work, leisure, and personal pursuits more effectively.

5. **Environmental Sustainability:** With increasing awareness of environmental issues, the sustainable use of resources and responsible consumption are integral aspects of contemporary wealth. Individuals who actively contribute to a healthier planet by making eco-conscious choices are seen as stewards of both their personal well-being and the global environment.

Technological Influence on Wealth Redefinition: The digital revolution has played a pivotal role in reshaping the understanding of wealth. The advent of the internet, smartphones, and the sharing economy has democratized access to information, goods, and services. Online platforms and digital tools have enabled individuals to monetize their skills, connect with global markets, and create wealth from non-traditional sources.

E-commerce, freelancing, and content creation have empowered individuals to transform their passions into income streams. Moreover, the rise of cryptocurrencies and blockchain technology has introduced new avenues for financial inclusion and investment, challenging conventional notions of wealth storage and transfer.

The Pursuit of Happiness and Meaning: Central to the redefinition of wealth in the 21st century is the pursuit of happiness and personal fulfillment. The emphasis on well-being, purpose-driven work, and experiences over possessions reflects a shift away from materialism. Many individuals are seeking careers that align with their passions, values, and the greater good, recognizing that wealth is not only about financial gain but also about leading a meaningful life.

Challenges and Considerations: As society embraces this redefined notion of wealth, certain challenges and considerations emerge:

1. **Inequality:** The expanded definition of wealth underscores existing inequalities. Not everyone has equal access to education, healthcare, or opportunities to accumulate human and social capital. Addressing these disparities is essential for a more equitable society.

2. **Digital Divide:** While technology has enabled new pathways to wealth, the digital divide persists, leaving marginalized communities at a disadvantage. Bridging this gap is essential to ensure that everyone can participate in the evolving landscape of wealth creation.

3. **Environmental Impact:** As wealth encompasses sustainability, individuals and businesses must consider the environmental consequences of their actions. Balancing economic prosperity with ecological well-being is a complex challenge that requires innovative solutions.

Conclusion: A Holistic Approach to Abundance: In conclusion, redefining wealth in the 21st century reflects a shift towards a more holistic and inclusive understanding of abundance. It encompasses diverse elements such as human capital, social connections, health, time, and sustainability. This multidimensional concept acknowledges the interplay between individual well-being, societal progress, and global harmony. As society continues to evolve, embracing this expanded definition of wealth can lead to a more balanced and fulfilling existence, where personal prosperity coexists with the greater good.

CHAPTER 3: THE MINDSET SHIFT: FROM SCARCITY TO ABUNDANCE

Introduction: The transition from a mindset of scarcity to one of abundance is a profound cognitive shift that shapes individuals' perceptions, decisions, and overall outlook on life. Rooted in psychology, philosophy, and personal development, this transformation represents a departure from the notion of lack and constraint toward embracing the idea of limitless potential and fulfillment. In a world often characterized by competition and fear, adopting an abundance mindset empowers individuals to approach challenges with resilience, gratitude, and a proactive spirit.

Understanding Scarcity and Abundance Mindsets: The scarcity mindset is characterized by a belief that resources, opportunities, and success are finite and limited. Individuals with this mindset often focus on what they lack, leading to fear of failure, comparison with others, and risk aversion. Conversely, the abundance mindset is marked by the belief that opportunities are abundant, and success is attainable through effort, creativity, and collaboration. Those with an abundance mindset tend to view challenges as opportunities for growth, cultivate gratitude, and readily embrace change.

The Cognitive Science Behind Mindset Shift: The psychology behind shifting from scarcity to abundance involves cognitive restructuring and reframing thought patterns. Neuroplasticity, the brain's ability to reorganize itself, plays a role in rewiring negative thought loops associated with scarcity. Practices like mindfulness, positive affirmations, and cognitive behavioral therapy contribute to this rewiring process, fostering an outlook that perceives abundance even in challenging circumstances.

Cultivating an Abundance Mindset:

1. **Gratitude Practice:** Gratitude is a cornerstone of the abundance mindset. Recognizing and appreciating the blessings, opportunities, and small victories in life reframes the narrative from scarcity to abundance.

2. **Embracing Change:** An abundance mindset sees change as an inevitable part of life that brings new possibilities. Embracing change fosters adaptability and reduces the fear of the unknown.

3. **Positive Self-Talk:** Being conscious of self-talk and transforming negative self-dialogue into positive affirmations enhances self-esteem and fosters a sense of empowerment.

4. **Taking Calculated Risks:** Embracing calculated risks becomes easier with an abundance mindset, as individuals believe in their capacity to rebound from setbacks and create new opportunities.

5. **Collaboration and Networking:** An abundance mindset encourages collaboration and networking, recognizing that cooperation creates win-win scenarios rather than perpetuating a scarcity-driven competition.

Applications in Personal and Professional Spheres:

1. **Career and Entrepreneurship:** Individuals with an abundance mindset seek innovative solutions, take on leadership roles, and embrace challenges in their careers and entrepreneurial endeavors. This approach promotes continuous learning, risk-taking, and resilience.

2. **Relationships:** Abundance thinking transforms relationships by focusing on support, empathy, and shared growth. It replaces jealousy and comparison with celebration of others' successes.

3. **Financial Well-being:** An abundance mindset encourages proactive financial planning and investment, confident that opportunities for growth

and prosperity are available.

Challenges and Obstacles: Transitioning to an abundance mindset is not without challenges, as deeply ingrained scarcity beliefs can be resistant to change. External factors like societal pressures, past experiences, and negative influences can hinder the shift. Consistent effort and commitment are required to overcome these obstacles.

Impact on Societal Progress: Embracing an abundance mindset on a collective level can lead to positive societal changes. Collaboration, innovation, and shared progress become central values, potentially reducing disparities, promoting sustainable practices, and fostering a more supportive and inclusive society.

Conclusion: The journey from scarcity to abundance is transformative and impactful. It entails reprogramming thought patterns, fostering gratitude, embracing change, and seeking growth opportunities. By adopting an abundance mindset, individuals not only enhance their personal well-being but also contribute to a broader culture of collaboration, resilience, and the realization of untapped potential. This shift represents a fundamental reimagining of the human experience, inviting individuals to see the world as a realm of endless possibilities.

CHAPTER 4: EMBRACING ENTREPRENEURIAL THINKING FOR FINANCIAL SUCCESS

Introduction: Entrepreneurial thinking, once confined to the realm of business startups, has now become a valuable mindset applicable to various aspects of life. This mode of thinking transcends the boundaries of entrepreneurship to empower individuals in pursuing financial success, regardless of their professional backgrounds. Grounded in innovation, adaptability, risk-taking, and strategic vision, embracing entrepreneurial thinking can catalyze not only personal financial growth but also foster a holistic approach to life's challenges.

Understanding Entrepreneurial Thinking: Entrepreneurial thinking goes beyond starting a business; it's about cultivating an innovative and proactive mindset characterized by several key traits:

1. **Innovation:** Entrepreneurs seek to solve problems and meet needs through creative solutions. Similarly, adopting an entrepreneurial mindset involves identifying opportunities for improvement and innovation in various spheres of life.

2. **Adaptability:** Entrepreneurs thrive in dynamic environments. Adopting an entrepreneurial mindset means being comfortable with change and willing to adjust strategies when circumstances shift.

3. **Risk-Taking:** Entrepreneurs are known for embracing calculated risks. Similarly, those who embrace entrepreneurial thinking recognize that taking calculated risks is essential for growth and seizing opportunities.

4. **Resilience:** Entrepreneurship is often marked by

setbacks. Embracing an entrepreneurial mindset involves developing resilience in the face of challenges, learning from failures, and bouncing back stronger.

5. **Strategic Vision:** Entrepreneurs set clear goals and develop strategies to achieve them. This approach to thinking involves setting financial goals, creating actionable plans, and working diligently toward success.

Applying Entrepreneurial Thinking for Financial Success:

1. **Identifying Opportunities:** Entrepreneurs spot gaps in the market. Similarly, embracing entrepreneurial thinking involves recognizing niches or untapped areas where financial success can be achieved.

2. **Diversifying Income Streams:** Entrepreneurs understand the importance of multiple revenue sources. Applying this mindset means exploring various income streams, investments, and side hustles to build financial stability.

3. **Continuous Learning:** Entrepreneurs constantly seek knowledge to stay competitive. Similarly, adopting entrepreneurial thinking entails ongoing learning about financial literacy, investment strategies, and economic trends.

4. **Networking and Collaboration:** Entrepreneurs build valuable networks. Likewise, individuals with an entrepreneurial mindset connect with others, seek mentorship, and collaborate to expand financial opportunities.

5. **Problem-Solving:** Entrepreneurs solve market problems. Applying this mindset involves identifying financial challenges and finding innovative solutions to overcome them.

Benefits and Challenges:

- **Benefits:** Embracing entrepreneurial thinking can lead

to increased financial independence, adaptability to changing economic landscapes, and the ability to capitalize on emerging trends. It promotes a proactive approach to achieving financial goals.

- **Challenges:** While the benefits are substantial, adopting an entrepreneurial mindset requires dedication and resilience. Overcoming fear of failure, balancing risk-taking, and maintaining consistent effort can be challenging.

Impact Beyond Finances: Embracing entrepreneurial thinking extends beyond financial success:

1. **Personal Growth:** Entrepreneurial thinking nurtures personal growth by encouraging individuals to step out of their comfort zones, challenge themselves, and develop new skills.

2. **Innovation:** Applying an entrepreneurial mindset to various aspects of life fosters innovative thinking and encourages individuals to find creative solutions to everyday problems.

3. **Empowerment:** Entrepreneurial thinking empowers individuals to take control of their financial future and make informed decisions that align with their goals.

4. **Mindset Shift:** Embracing entrepreneurial thinking shifts one's perspective from a passive consumer to an active creator of opportunities, enhancing self-confidence and autonomy.

Conclusion: Embracing entrepreneurial thinking for financial success is a transformative journey. It involves cultivating innovation, embracing change, taking calculated risks, and pursuing strategic visions. This mindset shift not only facilitates financial growth but also instills a sense of empowerment, resilience, and adaptability that extends far beyond monetary gains. By nurturing entrepreneurial thinking, individuals can navigate the complexities of the modern world with confidence, unlocking their potential for both financial prosperity and personal fulfillment.

CHAPTER 5: THE POWER OF INNOVATIVE DISRUPTION IN WEALTH CREATION

Introduction: In the dynamic landscape of wealth creation, the concept of innovative disruption has emerged as a transformative force that reshapes industries, drives economic growth, and empowers individuals to create substantial wealth. Rooted in the fusion of innovation and disruption, this phenomenon challenges traditional business models, fosters the emergence of new markets, and opens avenues for both established players and aspiring entrepreneurs. The power of innovative disruption lies in its ability to revolutionize existing paradigms, ignite opportunities, and ultimately redefine the path to financial success.

Understanding Innovative Disruption: Innovative disruption represents a seismic shift caused by the introduction of groundbreaking technologies, novel business models, or unconventional strategies. Coined by Clayton Christensen, this term encapsulates the idea that innovative advancements can disrupt established industries and markets, rendering previous norms obsolete. Disruptive innovations often cater to underserved or overlooked segments, offering simpler, more affordable, or more convenient solutions that challenge incumbents.

The Mechanisms of Innovative Disruption: Innovative disruption is driven by several key mechanisms:

1. **Technological Advancements:** Breakthrough technologies, such as artificial intelligence, blockchain, and renewable energy, pave the way for revolutionary changes in various sectors, fostering new opportunities for wealth creation.

2. **Market Entry Strategies:** Disruptors enter markets with disruptive business models that offer unique value propositions. These models can challenge incumbents by providing cost-effective alternatives or catering to previously untapped needs.

3. **Consumer Behavior Shifts:** Changing consumer preferences and demands can trigger disruption. Entrepreneurs who accurately predict and adapt to these shifts often gain a competitive advantage.

4. **Digitization and Connectivity:** The digital revolution has fueled the expansion of disruptive innovations. Connected ecosystems, data analytics, and e-commerce platforms have changed the way industries operate and consumers interact.

Disruption's Impact on Wealth Creation:

1. **Unleashing Entrepreneurial Potential:** Innovative disruption levels the playing field, enabling startups and small businesses to compete with larger players. Entrepreneurs who harness disruptive technologies can quickly gain market share and create substantial wealth.

2. **Creating New Markets:** Disruptive innovations often create entirely new markets by addressing unmet needs. This presents opportunities for early adopters to establish themselves as pioneers and market leaders.

3. **Wealth Redistribution:** Disruption can redistribute wealth from traditional industries to newer, more innovative sectors. This can lead to a democratization of wealth creation as more individuals have access to previously untapped opportunities.

4. **Encouraging Investment:** Disruptive industries attract investments from venture capitalists, angel investors, and even traditional players seeking to stay relevant. This injection of capital fuels growth and wealth

creation.

Examples of Disruptive Wealth Creation:

1. **Fintech Revolution:** The financial technology sector has transformed traditional banking and investment models, giving rise to innovative platforms for peer-to-peer lending, robo-advisors, and digital payments.

2. **E-Commerce Evolution:** Companies like Amazon have revolutionized retail by leveraging e-commerce and logistics, creating opportunities for entrepreneurs to tap into global markets.

3. **Sharing Economy:** The sharing economy, exemplified by platforms like Airbnb and Uber, has disrupted the hospitality and transportation industries, allowing individuals to monetize their assets.

4. **Renewable Energy:** Innovations in renewable energy technologies have led to the creation of sustainable solutions and investment opportunities in solar, wind, and other clean energy sources.

Challenges and Considerations: While innovative disruption presents numerous opportunities, challenges include:

1. **Resistance to Change:** Incumbent players may resist disruptive changes, leading to regulatory hurdles or market resistance.

2. **Uncertainty:** The fast-paced nature of disruptive markets can lead to uncertainty and volatility, requiring adaptive strategies.

3. **Ethical Implications:** Some disruptions can raise ethical concerns, such as data privacy or job displacement. Balancing innovation with social responsibility is essential.

Conclusion: The power of innovative disruption in wealth creation is a testament to human ingenuity and the ever-evolving nature of industries. By challenging established norms, harnessing new technologies, and adapting to changing consumer behaviors, individuals and businesses can unlock unprecedented opportunities for financial success. While disruptive innovation reshapes markets and empowers entrepreneurs, it also demands strategic foresight, adaptability, and a commitment to responsible wealth creation. As innovative disruptions continue to reshape industries, the path to financial success becomes a dynamic journey that rewards innovation, agility, and a keen eye for emerging trends.

CHAPTER 6: NAVIGATING THE DIGITAL LANDSCAPE: TECHNOLOGY AND WEALTH

Introduction: In the 21st century, the rapid advancement of technology has revolutionized nearly every aspect of our lives, including the way we create, manage, and accumulate wealth. The digital landscape has become an intricate tapestry where innovation, connectivity, and opportunities intersect to shape new paradigms of wealth generation and management. Navigating this landscape requires an understanding of how technology influences wealth creation, the impact on traditional industries, the rise of digital assets, and the importance of digital literacy in achieving financial success.

Technology as a Catalyst for Wealth Creation: Technology has democratized access to information, markets, and resources, creating an environment where innovative ideas can flourish. It has significantly lowered the barriers to entry for entrepreneurs and creators, enabling individuals to leverage digital platforms for business and creative ventures. E-commerce, social media, and online marketplaces have opened global markets to small businesses and individuals, allowing them to reach a broader audience and generate wealth on a scale that was previously unimaginable.

Disruption and Transformation of Traditional Industries: Digital transformation has disrupted traditional industries, challenged established-business models and paved the way for new economic landscapes. Sectors like finance, healthcare, and education have been reshaped by fintech, telemedicine, and online learning platforms, respectively. This disruption not only creates opportunities for innovative startups but also demands adaptability from existing players to remain competitive in the digital age.

Cryptocurrencies and Digital Assets: The emergence of cryptocurrencies and digital assets has introduced a new dimension to the digital landscape of wealth. Cryptocurrencies like Bitcoin and Ethereum have gained attention as alternative forms of investment and stores of value. Decentralized finance (DeFi) platforms leverage blockchain technology to offer financial services such as lending, borrowing, and trading, without traditional intermediaries. The potential for high returns has attracted investors seeking diversification and exposure to digital assets.

Wealth Management in the Digital Age: Digital technology has transformed wealth management, making it more accessible and personalized. Robo-advisors use algorithms to create investment portfolios tailored to individual risk profiles and financial goals. Mobile banking apps offer real-time financial insights, budgeting tools, and investment tracking. Additionally, online brokerage platforms enable individuals to invest in stocks, bonds, and funds with ease, reducing the need for traditional financial intermediaries.

Digital Literacy and Financial Empowerment: Navigating the digital landscape requires a certain level of digital literacy. Individuals must understand concepts like cybersecurity, data privacy, and online scams to protect their wealth in a digital world. Financial education has also become increasingly important, as digital platforms offer an array of investment options that require informed decision-making. Empowering individuals with digital literacy equip them to make sound financial choices and avoid potential pitfalls.

Challenges and Ethical Considerations: While technology offers immense potential for wealth creation, it also poses challenges and ethical considerations:

1. **Digital Divide:** Not everyone has equal access to technology, creating a digital divide that can exacerbate socioeconomic disparities.

2. **Privacy and Security:** The digital landscape raises concerns about data privacy, online fraud, and cybersecurity threats that can compromise financial well-being.

3. **Ethical Tech Use:** The ethical use of technology in wealth creation involves responsible AI, addressing biases, and considering social impact.

Conclusion: Navigating the digital landscape of technology and wealth requires a proactive and adaptable mindset. The integration of technology into wealth creation and management offers unprecedented opportunities for entrepreneurship, investment, and financial empowerment. However, it also demands a commitment to digital literacy, responsible tech use, and ethical considerations. As the digital landscape continues to evolve, those who embrace technology's potential while remaining vigilant and informed will be best positioned to harness its power for personal and societal wealth advancement in the 21st century.

CHAPTER 7: UNMASKING INVESTMENT OPPORTUNITIES IN THE INFORMATION AGE

Introduction: The Information Age has ushered in an era of unprecedented connectivity, digital transformation, and data proliferation. Amidst this landscape, investment opportunities have expanded far beyond traditional avenues, evolving to incorporate technology-driven platforms, innovative startups, and data-driven strategies. To succeed in unmasking these opportunities, individuals must navigate an intricate web of information, harness emerging technologies, and cultivate a deep understanding of market trends. This exploration delves into the dynamics of investment in the Information Age, uncovering the methods to identify, evaluate, and capitalize on opportunities that hold the potential for substantial wealth accumulation.

Data-Driven Insights and Investment Strategies: In the Information Age, data is a powerful asset that provides insights into market trends, consumer behavior, and emerging sectors. Investors can leverage data analytics and artificial intelligence to make informed decisions. Machine learning algorithms analyze vast amounts of data to identify patterns, helping investors predict market movements and allocate resources more effectively.

Startups and Disruptive Innovation: The Information Age has birthed a plethora of startups leveraging innovative technologies to disrupt traditional industries. From fintech and biotech to renewable energy and e-commerce, these startups challenge established norms, presenting investment opportunities with high growth potential. Early-stage investments in startups can yield substantial returns if successful, making angel investing and venture capital a vital part of modern investment strategies.

Cryptocurrencies and Blockchain Technology: The emergence of cryptocurrencies and blockchain technology has revolutionized the financial landscape. Cryptocurrencies like Bitcoin and Ethereum have gained recognition as alternative assets with potential for high returns. Additionally, blockchain's transparent and secure nature has found applications beyond cryptocurrency, disrupting industries such as supply chain management, real estate, and healthcare.

E-Commerce and Digital Marketplaces: E-commerce platforms and digital marketplaces have transformed the retail industry, offering new investment horizons. Beyond well-known platforms, opportunities lie in niche e-commerce markets, dropshipping, and online marketplaces that cater to specific interests or demographics. The rise of direct-to-consumer brands also presents avenues for investment in digitally native products and services.

Renewable Energy and Sustainability: The global shift towards sustainability has led to investment opportunities in renewable energy sources such as solar, wind, and hydroelectric power. Technological advancements and governmental incentives create a favorable environment for investing in clean energy, which not only generates returns but also contributes to a greener future.

Real Estate and Proptech Innovation: Real estate investment has also evolved in the Information Age with the rise of proptech (property technology). Crowdfunding platforms and online marketplaces democratize real estate investment, allowing individuals to invest in properties without the need for large capital commitments. Proptech innovations, such as smart homes and real estate analytics, enhance the potential for lucrative returns.

Challenges and Considerations: Unmasking investment opportunities in the Information Age comes with challenges:

1. **Information Overload:** The abundance of information can lead to information paralysis. Investors must filter

through vast data to identify relevant insights.

2. **Technological Risks:** Investing in emerging technologies carries risks, including regulatory uncertainties and potential for rapid market fluctuations.

3. **Digital Security:** As investment activities move online, cybersecurity becomes crucial to protect sensitive financial information.

Conclusion: Unmasking investment opportunities in the Information Age requires a dynamic blend of data-driven insights, technological acumen, and adaptability. The landscape is diverse, encompassing startups, disruptive technologies, alternative assets, and sustainable ventures. Success in this realm demands continuous learning, a proactive approach to embracing innovation, and an understanding of evolving market trends. By harnessing the power of information, staying informed about technological advancements, and maintaining a forward-thinking mindset, investors can navigate the complexities of the Information Age to uncover opportunities that hold the promise of significant wealth accumulation.

CHAPTER 8: LEVERAGING THE GLOBAL MARKETPLACE: THE NEW RULES OF TRADE

Introduction: In an era of globalization and interconnectedness, the global marketplace has become a dynamic ecosystem that transcends geographical boundaries. The advent of advanced communication technologies, logistics networks, and digital platforms has reshaped the rules of trade. The new landscape offers immense opportunities for businesses, entrepreneurs, and economies to leverage international markets and drive economic growth. This exploration delves into the intricacies of the global marketplace, uncovering its transformative impact, the evolving rules of engagement, challenges, and strategies to effectively navigate this dynamic arena.

Globalization's Transformative Impact: Globalization has led to the interdependence of economies, fueled by the free flow of goods, services, information, and capital. This interconnectedness has elevated the concept of the global marketplace from a theoretical notion to a tangible reality. Cross-border trade has facilitated the exchange of diverse products, ideas, and cultures, enriching societies and economies alike. The global marketplace has become a hub of innovation, collaboration, and opportunity for those who understand its nuances.

Evolving Rules of Engagement:

1. **Digital Disruption:** Technology has revolutionized commerce, enabling businesses of all sizes to access international markets. E-commerce platforms, digital payment systems, and online marketplaces have created a borderless environment for trade.

2. **Trade Agreements and Treaties:** Bilateral and

multilateral trade agreements, such as free trade agreements (FTAs), promote the reduction of trade barriers and tariffs, facilitating smoother cross-border transactions.

3. **Intellectual Property Protection:** As ideas and innovations are shared globally, robust intellectual property protection is essential. International agreements like TRIPS (Trade-Related Aspects of Intellectual Property Rights) ensure that creators' rights are upheld.

4. **Logistics and Supply Chain:** Efficient logistics networks, including transportation and warehousing, are critical for successful global trade. Advances in supply chain management enhance the movement of goods across borders.

Strategies for Navigating the Global Marketplace:

1. **Market Research and Localization:** Understanding local cultures, preferences, and regulatory landscapes is vital. Customizing products, services, and marketing strategies to suit each market increases the chances of success.

2. **E-Commerce and Digital Marketing:** Leveraging digital platforms allows businesses to reach global audiences with minimal overhead costs. Effective digital marketing strategies enable targeted outreach.

3. **Diversification and Risk Mitigation:** Relying on a single market can be risky. Diversification across multiple markets reduces vulnerability to economic fluctuations in a single region.

4. **Partnerships and Alliances:** Collaborations with local partners, distributors, and suppliers provide insights into foreign markets and help navigate legal and cultural complexities.

5. **Compliance and Regulation:** Navigating international trade requires adherence to various regulations and compliance standards. Staying updated on local laws is essential to avoid legal complications.

Challenges in the Global Marketplace:

1. **Cultural Sensitivity:** Cultural differences can impact communication, marketing, and business practices. Failing to understand local customs may lead to misunderstandings or failures.

2. **Political and Economic Instability:** Unpredictable political environments and economic fluctuations in foreign markets can affect trade stability.

3. **Logistical Challenges:** International shipping, customs procedures, and regulatory compliance can lead to logistical complexities and delays.

4. **Trade Barriers and Tariffs:** Despite trade agreements, some regions impose tariffs and trade barriers that increase costs and limit market access.

Conclusion: Leveraging the global marketplace in the modern age demands a nuanced understanding of evolving trade dynamics. The transformative impact of globalization has birthed a borderless world of opportunities and challenges. Businesses and individuals who can adapt to new rules of engagement, embrace technological advancements, and navigate cultural, regulatory, and logistical complexities stand to benefit significantly. As the global marketplace continues to evolve, those who seize the opportunities it presents while strategizing to overcome its challenges will be best positioned to drive economic growth, foster innovation, and capitalize on the vast potential of interconnected markets.

CHAPTER 9: THE SOCIAL CAPITAL PARADIGM: NETWORKING YOUR WAY TO MILLIONS

Introduction: In the journey towards financial success and wealth creation, the significance of relationships cannot be overstated. The social capital paradigm recognizes that beyond financial resources, connections and networks play a pivotal role in opening doors, fostering opportunities, and propelling individuals towards achieving their financial goals. This exploration delves into the depths of the social capital paradigm, unveiling how networking, relationship-building, and collaboration serve as catalysts for wealth accumulation, innovation, and personal growth.

Understanding Social Capital: Social capital is an intangible asset that encompasses the networks, relationships, and connections individuals cultivate over time. It encompasses both strong ties (close relationships) and weak ties (acquaintances) that collectively contribute to an individual's access to resources, information, and opportunities. Building social capital requires genuine interactions, trust, reciprocity, and a commitment to mutual benefit.

The Role of Networking: Networking is a cornerstone of the social capital paradigm. It involves deliberately cultivating relationships within professional and personal spheres to create a supportive ecosystem. Effective networking goes beyond transactional interactions; it involves fostering genuine connections, adding value to others, and consistently nurturing relationships over time.

Leveraging Relationships for Wealth Creation:

1. **Access to Opportunities:** Well-connected individuals have access to a broader range of opportunities,

from business partnerships and investment ventures to career advancements.

2. **Innovation and Knowledge Exchange:** Social capital fosters the exchange of ideas, insights, and knowledge across diverse fields, spurring innovation and creative problem-solving.

3. **Resource Mobilization:** When individuals have a robust network, they can leverage it for resource mobilization, whether it's funding, expertise, or support.

4. **Market Expansion:** Building relationships with diverse stakeholders allows for market expansion, enabling businesses to tap into new customer bases and demographics.

Strategies for Effective Networking:

1. **Authenticity:** Genuine connections are built on authenticity and mutual respect. Being sincere in interactions fosters trust and credibility.

2. **Active Listening:** Listening attentively and showing a genuine interest in others strengthens connections and demonstrates respect.

3. **Reciprocity:** Building social capital involves giving as much as receiving. Offering help, sharing insights, and offering support builds goodwill.

4. **Maintaining Relationships:** Consistently nurturing relationships through communication and follow-ups is essential for sustaining social capital.

Digital Age and Social Capital: In the digital age, technology has amplified the scope of social capital. Social media platforms enable individuals to connect with a global audience, creating opportunities for collaborations and networking on an unprecedented scale. However, while digital platforms can facilitate initial connections, cultivating meaningful relationships still relies on genuine interactions and trust-building.

The Broader Impact:

1. **Personal Growth:** Beyond wealth creation, social capital contributes to personal growth, enhancing communication skills, empathy, and adaptability.

2. **Community Building:** Social capital fosters a sense of community and belonging, as individuals come together to support each other's endeavors.

3. **Social Impact:** Well-networked individuals often use their influence to drive positive change, whether through philanthropy, advocacy, or entrepreneurship.

Challenges and Ethical Considerations:

1. **Network Maintenance:** Balancing the maintenance of relationships across diverse networks can be challenging, requiring time management and prioritization.

2. **Authenticity:** Building social capital must stem from genuine intentions rather than solely seeking personal gain.

3. **Inclusivity:** While networking, it's important to consider diversity and inclusion, ensuring a variety of perspectives are represented within one's network.

Conclusion: The social capital paradigm illuminates the fact that success in wealth creation and personal growth is not solely about individual prowess, but also about the strength of one's connections and relationships. Navigating the intricate web of social capital involves cultivating authentic networks, adding value to others, and harnessing the collective power of collaboration. In the ever-evolving landscape of finance and business, those who understand the power of relationships and prioritize the cultivation of social capital will be better positioned to harness opportunities, catalyze innovation, and ultimately unlock the path to financial success and personal fulfillment.

CHAPTER 10: EDUCATION RENAISSANCE: LEARNING AND EARNING IN SYNERGY

Introduction: The concept of education has transcended its traditional boundaries and evolved into a dynamic process that extends beyond classrooms and textbooks. In the midst of the digital age, an "Education Renaissance" is underway – a paradigm shift that emphasizes the symbiotic relationship between learning and earning. This transformative movement highlights how continuous education, skill development, and knowledge acquisition are not only essential for personal growth but also serve as catalysts for professional success, innovation, and economic advancement. This exploration delves into the intricacies of the Education Renaissance, unveiling the ways in which learning and earning synergistically drive individual prosperity and societal progress.

The Changing Landscape of Education: The Education Renaissance is marked by a departure from the conventional education model, which often ends with formal schooling. Lifelong learning has emerged as a cornerstone, driven by the rapid pace of technological advancement and the ever-evolving nature of industries. The rise of online learning platforms, microcredentials, and skill-based courses enables individuals to continuously upskill and adapt to changing demands, creating a cycle of perpetual learning.

Learning and Earning in Synergy:

1. **Skill Relevance:** In a rapidly evolving job market, acquiring new skills and staying updated is crucial for employability. Learning enhances an individual's ability to contribute effectively in their chosen field, driving career growth.

2. **Career Resilience:** The Education Renaissance fosters career resilience by enabling professionals to pivot and adapt as industries transform. Learning ensures that individuals remain competitive and relevant in their chosen domains.

3. **Entrepreneurial Pursuits:** Learning extends beyond traditional employment; it empowers aspiring entrepreneurs to acquire the knowledge and skills needed to launch and sustain successful ventures.

4. **Innovation and Creativity:** Continuous learning nurtures innovative thinking and creative problem-solving. Professionals who constantly seek knowledge are better equipped to develop groundbreaking solutions.

Education and Economic Advancement:

1. **Economic Growth:** The Education Renaissance contributes to economic growth by supplying a skilled workforce and fostering innovation, both of which drive productivity and competitiveness.

2. **Job Creation:** As individuals develop expertise in emerging fields, they create demand for specialized roles, leading to job creation and industry expansion.

3. **Global Competitiveness:** Countries that prioritize education and lifelong learning enhance their global competitiveness, attracting investments and talent.

The Digital Learning Revolution: Online learning platforms and digital resources have democratized education, making learning accessible to a global audience. Learners can choose from a vast array of courses tailored to their interests, schedules, and career aspirations. The rise of Massive Open Online Courses (MOOCs), webinars, and virtual workshops enables individuals to learn from experts regardless of geographical constraints.

Challenges and Considerations:

1. **Affordability and Access:** While digital education is accessible, concerns about affordability and access persist, particularly for marginalized communities with limited internet connectivity.

2. **Credential Recognition:** As non-traditional forms of education gain prominence, there's a need for standardized methods of credential recognition to ensure the value of acquired skills.

3. **Learning Overload:** The abundance of learning opportunities can lead to "learning overload," where individuals struggle to prioritize and retain information effectively.

Conclusion: The Education Renaissance underscores the inseparable link between learning and earning. It paints a picture of education as a continuous journey, where knowledge acquisition becomes a lifelong pursuit that enhances not only personal growth but also economic prosperity. In this age of perpetual innovation, embracing the synergistic relationship between learning and earning is essential for individuals, industries, and societies. The collective embrace of lifelong learning has the potential to propel us into a future characterized by empowered professionals, dynamic economies, and a culture of innovation that paves the way for an era of unprecedented progress and success.

CHAPTER 11: THE ART OF ADAPTIVE RISK-TAKING: CALCULATED VENTURES

Introduction: In the dynamic landscape of personal and professional growth, the art of adaptive risk-taking stands as a defining trait of individuals and organizations that achieve remarkable innovation and success. Adaptive risk-taking involves the deliberate and calculated pursuit of opportunities that carry an element of uncertainty. This strategic approach to risk acknowledges that stepping outside one's comfort zone and embracing uncertainty can lead to breakthroughs, resilience, and substantial rewards. This exploration delves into the nuances of adaptive risk-taking, its psychological underpinnings, strategies for effective implementation, its role in fostering innovation, and the balance between boldness and prudence.

Understanding Adaptive Risk-Taking: Adaptive risk-taking is not recklessness; rather, it involves a systematic assessment of potential outcomes, informed decision-making, and a willingness to learn from failures. It requires individuals to acknowledge that growth and innovation often stem from stepping into uncharted territories, challenging the status quo, and being open to unexpected outcomes.

Psychology of Risk-Taking:

1. **Cognitive Appraisal:** Adaptive risk-takers engage in cognitive appraisal, evaluating the potential gains, losses, and consequences of a decision. They weigh the rewards against the perceived risks.

2. **Tolerance for Ambiguity:** Those adept at adaptive risk-taking possess a higher tolerance for ambiguity and uncertainty. They view ambiguity as an opportunity to explore uncharted territory.

3. **Growth Mindset:** A growth mindset, emphasizing the

belief that abilities can be developed through effort and learning, contributes to adaptive risk-taking. Failure is seen as a chance to learn and improve.

Strategies for Effective Adaptive Risk-Taking:

1. **Informed Decision-Making:** Conduct thorough research and gather relevant information before making decisions. Understanding the context and potential outcomes helps mitigate blind spots.

2. **Risk Diversification:** Diversify risk by spreading investments or efforts across different ventures. This approach minimizes the impact of potential failures.

3. **Calculating Risk-Reward Ratio:** Assess the potential rewards against the perceived risks. A balanced risk-reward ratio guides decision-making toward ventures with a higher chance of success.

4. **Learning from Failures:** Embrace failures as valuable learning experiences. Analyze what went wrong, extract insights, and apply these lessons to future endeavors.

Adaptive Risk-Taking and Innovation:

1. **Catalyst for Innovation:** Innovation often emerges from pushing boundaries and exploring uncharted territories. Adaptive risk-takers drive innovation by challenging conventional norms.

2. **Embracing Uncertainty:** The uncertain nature of adaptive risk-taking fuels creative thinking and problem-solving. It encourages individuals to find unique solutions to unforeseen challenges.

3. **Competitive Advantage:** Organizations that foster a culture of adaptive risk-taking gain a competitive edge. They are more agile, responsive to market changes, and better positioned to seize emerging opportunities.

Balancing Boldness and Prudence:

1. **Overcoming Paralysis:** While calculated risk-taking is essential, excessive caution can lead to missed opportunities and stagnation. Finding the balance between boldness and prudence is key.

2. **Assessing Impact:** Consider the potential impact of a risk on various aspects, including personal, financial, and emotional. Mitigate risks that could have catastrophic consequences.

Challenges and Ethical Considerations:

1. **Ethical Boundaries:** Adaptive risk-taking should operate within ethical boundaries, avoiding actions that could harm individuals, communities, or the environment.

2. **Overconfidence Bias:** Individuals may overestimate their ability to manage risk, leading to rash decisions. Self-awareness is crucial in combating overconfidence bias.

Conclusion: The art of adaptive risk-taking is a hallmark of individuals and organizations that embrace growth, innovation, and resilience. Through a combination of informed decision-making, calculated strategies, and a willingness to learn from failures, adaptive risk-takers navigate uncertainty and create pathways to success. As technology, markets, and industries continue to evolve, those who master the art of adaptive risk-taking stand to harness unprecedented opportunities, shape their destinies, and leave a lasting legacy of transformative innovation.

CHAPTER 12: SUSTAINABILITY AND PROFITABILITY: THE GREEN WEALTH MOVEMENT

Introduction: The modern era has witnessed a paradigm shift in the way individuals, businesses, and societies approach the concepts of sustainability and profitability. The Green Wealth Movement is an embodiment of this shift, emphasizing that sustainability and profitability are not mutually exclusive but rather can coexist harmoniously. This movement acknowledges that responsible environmental practices can drive economic growth, enhance social well-being, and create a more equitable and resilient future. This exploration delves into the multifaceted landscape of the Green Wealth Movement, unveiling its key principles, the business case for sustainable practices, societal implications, and strategies for fostering a thriving, eco-conscious global economy.

Understanding the Green Wealth Movement: The Green Wealth Movement is grounded in the belief that environmental stewardship and economic prosperity can go hand in hand. It recognizes that the pursuit of wealth should be aligned with responsible resource management, reduced carbon emissions, conservation of natural habitats, and sustainable development. This movement is characterized by a commitment to creating value for present and future generations by incorporating environmental considerations into economic decision-making.

The Business Case for Sustainability:

1. **Cost Efficiency:** Sustainable practices often lead to cost savings in the long run. Energy-efficient operations, waste reduction, and responsible resource management contribute to lower operational expenses.

2. **Innovation and Competitive Advantage:** Embracing

sustainability encourages innovation, leading to the development of eco-friendly products, services, and processes that can differentiate businesses in the market.

3. **Customer Demand:** Increasingly conscious consumers are demanding products and services that align with their values. Companies that prioritize sustainability are more likely to attract and retain customers.

4. **Regulatory Compliance:** Governments worldwide are implementing stricter environmental regulations. Companies that proactively adopt sustainable practices are better positioned to comply with evolving standards.

Societal Implications and Well-Being:

1. **Equity and Inclusivity:** The Green Wealth Movement seeks to ensure that sustainability benefits all segments of society. It emphasizes inclusivity, creating green jobs, and reducing inequalities.

2. **Climate Resilience:** Investing in sustainable practices enhances societies' ability to withstand and adapt to the impacts of climate change, reducing vulnerabilities and minimizing disruptions.

3. **Health and Well-being:** A clean and healthy environment directly impacts public health. Reduced pollution, improved air quality, and access to green spaces contribute to better well-being.

Strategies for Green Wealth Creation:

1. **Sustainable Innovation:** Prioritize innovation that aligns with environmental goals. Develop products, technologies, and services that contribute to sustainable living.

2. **Supply Chain Sustainability:** Collaborate with suppliers and partners to ensure responsible sourcing, ethical labor practices, and reduced carbon footprint across the

supply chain.

3. **Circular Economy:** Embrace the principles of a circular economy, where resources are reused, repurposed, and recycled to minimize waste and maximize value.

4. **Transparency and Reporting:** Communicate sustainability efforts transparently to customers, investors, and stakeholders. Robust reporting demonstrates a commitment to responsible business practices.

Challenges and Considerations:

1. **Initial Costs:** Implementing sustainable practices may involve upfront costs. However, the long-term benefits often outweigh the initial investment.

2. **Behavioral Change:** Achieving the Green Wealth Movement requires a shift in individual and collective behaviors. Raising awareness and fostering environmentally conscious mindsets are essential.

3. **Global Cooperation:** Addressing environmental challenges requires international collaboration, as environmental issues transcend geographical boundaries.

Conclusion: The Green Wealth Movement embodies a vision of prosperity that values ecological sustainability alongside economic growth. By embracing sustainable practices, individuals, businesses, and societies can create a legacy of positive impact on the planet and its inhabitants. The movement demonstrates that profitability need not come at the expense of environmental degradation; instead, it showcases that green wealth is a holistic approach that nurtures the well-being of both people and the planet. As the world collectively strives for a sustainable future, the Green Wealth Movement stands as a guiding beacon, inspiring us to reshape our economic paradigms and embrace a new era of responsible prosperity.

CHAPTER 13: BEYOND TRADITIONAL BANKING: FINANCIAL EVOLUTION UNLEASHED

Introduction: The landscape of financial services has undergone a profound transformation, propelled by technological advancements, changing consumer behaviors, and the emergence of innovative fintech solutions. "Beyond Traditional Banking" signifies a seismic shift in how financial services are delivered, consumed, and perceived. This evolution encompasses a spectrum of innovations, from digital banking and blockchain technology to decentralized finance (DeFi) and artificial intelligence (AI)-driven financial solutions. This exploration delves deep into the facets of this financial evolution, illuminating the key drivers, transformative technologies, impact on traditional banking, regulatory considerations, and the journey towards a more inclusive and digitized financial future.

Drivers of Financial Evolution:

1. **Technological Advancements:** The advent of digital technologies, AI, blockchain, and data analytics has enabled the creation of new financial services and streamlined processes.

2. **Changing Consumer Expectations:** Consumers demand convenience, accessibility, and personalized financial services, pushing institutions to innovate and provide user-centric solutions.

3. **Fintech Innovation:** Fintech startups disrupt traditional banking models by offering innovative solutions in payments, lending, wealth management, and insurance.

Transformative Technologies:

1. **Digital Banking and Mobile Apps:** Traditional banking services are now available through digital platforms and mobile apps, offering 24/7 access, real-time transactions, and seamless user experiences.

2. **Blockchain and Cryptocurrencies:** Blockchain technology and cryptocurrencies like Bitcoin and Ethereum have introduced decentralized financial systems, offering transparency, security, and borderless transactions.

3. **Artificial Intelligence and Robo-Advisors:** AI-powered algorithms analyze data to provide personalized financial advice, manage investments, and automate routine tasks.

4. **Decentralized Finance (DeFi):** DeFi platforms leverage blockchain to offer financial services like lending, borrowing, and trading without intermediaries, promoting financial inclusion.

Impact on Traditional Banking:

1. **Competition and Collaboration:** Fintech startups compete with traditional banks, but collaboration also occurs as banks integrate fintech solutions into their services.

2. **Customer-Centric Approach:** The shift towards user-centric fintech solutions encourages traditional banks to enhance their customer experiences and digital offerings.

3. **Branch Transformation:** As digital banking gains prominence, traditional bank branches evolve to offer advisory services and specialized customer interactions.

Financial Inclusion and Empowerment:

1. **Global Reach:** Beyond traditional banking, fintech solutions can reach unbanked and underbanked populations worldwide, providing access to financial

services.

2. **Microtransactions:** Fintech enables microtransactions and microloans, catering to individuals with limited resources and promoting economic empowerment.

3. **Cross-Border Transactions:** Digital payments and cryptocurrencies facilitate cross-border transactions, eliminating the need for intermediaries and reducing costs.

Regulatory Considerations:

1. **Regulatory Innovation:** Governments and regulatory bodies are adapting to fintech advancements, establishing frameworks to ensure consumer protection, security, and privacy.

2. **Balancing Innovation and Risks:** Regulators seek to strike a balance between encouraging innovation and mitigating risks like money laundering, fraud, and cybersecurity threats.

Challenges and Ethical Implications:

1. **Data Privacy:** As digital financial services collect vast amounts of user data, ensuring data privacy and security remains a challenge.

2. **Digital Divide:** While fintech can promote financial inclusion, the digital divide can exclude those without access to technology.

3. **Ethical AI Use:** The integration of AI in financial services raises ethical questions about biases, transparency, and accountability.

Conclusion: The evolution beyond traditional banking represents a monumental shift in the financial services landscape. Technological innovations, changing consumer behaviors, and a commitment to financial inclusion are reshaping the industry. As we embrace a future where digital banking, blockchain,

AI-driven solutions, and DeFi platforms coexist, the financial evolution promises increased convenience, empowerment, and accessibility. Striking the right balance between innovation, regulation, and ethical considerations will pave the way for a more inclusive, interconnected, and resilient financial ecosystem that empowers individuals and businesses on a global scale.

CHAPTER 14: DATA GOLDMINE: TRANSFORMING INFORMATION INTO WEALTH

Introduction: In the digital age, data has emerged as a new form of wealth, often referred to as the "Data Goldmine." The proliferation of technology and the digitalization of various aspects of our lives have led to the generation of massive amounts of data. This data holds immense potential, as businesses and individuals alike recognize its value in driving insights, innovation, and ultimately, wealth creation. This exploration delves deep into the concept of the Data Goldmine, exploring its significance, the process of transforming data into wealth, ethical considerations, and the far-reaching implications for industries and economies.

The Value of Data: Data has become a valuable asset that can provide insights into consumer behavior, market trends, and operational efficiencies. Its potential lies in its ability to inform decision-making, enhance business strategies, and facilitate the creation of new products and services.

Data Monetization:

1. **Personal Data:** Individuals can monetize their personal data by participating in surveys, online reviews, and loyalty programs that reward them for sharing their preferences and behaviors.

2. **Business Insights:** Companies can monetize data by analyzing customer preferences, predicting market trends, and optimizing supply chains to gain a competitive edge.

3. **Data Marketplaces:** Data marketplaces enable individuals and organizations to buy, sell, and trade datasets, creating new revenue streams and fostering

collaboration.

Transforming Data into Wealth:

1. **Data Analysis:** The first step is to analyze the collected data to extract meaningful insights. Advanced analytics, machine learning, and artificial intelligence can uncover patterns and correlations.

2. **Informed Decision-Making:** Data-driven insights guide decision-making, helping businesses tailor strategies, refine marketing campaigns, and allocate resources more effectively.

3. **Innovation:** Data fosters innovation by identifying gaps in the market, uncovering emerging trends, and supporting the development of new products and services.

Data Privacy and Ethics:

1. **Privacy Concerns:** As data becomes more valuable, concerns about privacy and data protection grow. Striking a balance between data utilization and privacy is crucial.

2. **Consent and Transparency:** Ethical data utilization involves obtaining informed consent from individuals whose data is being used. Transparency in data collection and usage is essential.

3. **Avoiding Bias:** Analyzing data with fairness and avoiding biases is vital to ensure equitable outcomes and prevent perpetuation of existing inequalities.

Industry Implications:

1. **Marketing and Advertising:** Data-driven insights enable targeted marketing, personalized advertising, and the optimization of ad campaigns for better returns on investment.

2. **Healthcare:** Data analysis in healthcare can lead to more

accurate diagnoses, treatment recommendations, and drug development.

3. **Financial Services:** Data informs risk assessment, fraud detection, and the development of innovative financial products like robo-advisors.

4. **Smart Cities:** Data utilization can lead to the creation of smart cities with optimized infrastructure, transportation systems, and energy consumption.

Economic Growth and Innovation:

1. **Economic Contribution:** The Data Goldmine contributes to economic growth by creating new industries, jobs in data analysis, and opportunities for entrepreneurs.

2. **Innovation Ecosystem:** Data-driven innovation fuels the growth of startups and established businesses, promoting technological advancements and market disruption.

Conclusion: The Data Goldmine represents an era where data is not just a byproduct of technology but a valuable resource that can drive innovation, inform strategies, and create wealth. The transformation of data into wealth requires a balanced approach that considers ethical considerations, data privacy, and the potential for positive societal impact. As industries, economies, and societies continue to harness the power of data, the Data Goldmine holds the promise of reshaping how we approach business, innovation, and decision-making, driving us toward a more data-informed and prosperous future.

CHAPTER 15: CREATIVE CAPITAL: MONETIZING IDEAS AND INTELLECTUAL PROPERTY

Introduction: In the modern knowledge-based economy, the concept of wealth has expanded beyond tangible assets to encompass the realm of ideas and intellectual property. "Creative Capital" represents the transformation of innovative ideas, original creations, and intellectual prowess into valuable assets that can be monetized for financial gain. This paradigm shift recognizes that intellectual property, from patents and copyrights to trademarks and trade secrets, has the potential to generate substantial revenue and contribute significantly to economic growth. This exploration delves into the multifaceted landscape of creative capital, unveiling its significance, strategies for monetization, legal considerations, and its pivotal role in fostering innovation and prosperity.

Understanding Creative Capital: Creative capital encompasses the intangible assets born of human ingenuity, such as inventions, artistic works, literary compositions, and technological breakthroughs. This intellectual property holds inherent value that can be harnessed for financial gain, reflecting the shift from physical to knowledge-based wealth.

Monetization Strategies:

1. **Licensing and Royalties:** Intellectual property owners can license their creations to third parties in exchange for royalties, generating revenue while retaining ownership.

2. **Selling Intellectual Property:** Selling patents, copyrights, or trademarks outright to interested buyers can provide a lump sum payment.

3. **Commercialization:** Transforming inventions or ideas

into marketable products or services, whether through startups or established businesses, is a path to monetization.

4. **Content Creation:** Monetizing content, such as videos, articles, and online courses, through platforms like YouTube, Patreon, and Udemy, can generate income based on user engagement.

Legal Considerations:

1. **Copyrights:** Copyright protection applies to original literary, artistic, and musical works, granting creators exclusive rights to reproduce, distribute, and perform their creations.

2. **Trademarks:** Trademarks protect distinctive symbols, logos, and brand names, preventing others from using similar marks in a way that could cause confusion.

3. **Patents:** Patents grant inventors exclusive rights to their inventions, enabling them to control the production, sale, and use of the patented technology.

4. **Trade Secrets:** Intellectual property that provides a competitive advantage can be protected as trade secrets through nondisclosure agreements and other legal measures.

Fostering Innovation and Prosperity:

1. **Incentive for Innovation:** Intellectual property protection incentivizes innovators to invest time, effort, and resources in creating new technologies and solutions.

2. **Economic Growth:** Creative capital contributes to economic growth by fostering entrepreneurship, creating jobs, and driving the development of new industries.

3. **Technological Advancement:** Monetizing intellectual

property encourages the development of cutting-edge technologies, contributing to societal progress and competitiveness.

Challenges and Ethical Implications:

1. **Balancing Access and Ownership:** Striking a balance between encouraging innovation through intellectual property rights and ensuring access to essential knowledge is a challenge.

2. **Patent Trolling:** Some entities acquire patents solely to sue others for alleged infringement, stifling innovation and leading to legal disputes.

3. **Ethical Content Monetization:** Monetizing content raises ethical questions about user privacy, data collection, and the impact of monetization on content quality.

Conclusion: Creative capital is the bridge that connects ideas, innovation, and financial prosperity. In an age where knowledge is power, the ability to monetize intellectual property fuels economic growth, fosters innovation, and empowers individuals and businesses to leverage their ingenuity for financial gain. By understanding the legal frameworks, embracing ethical considerations, and strategically approaching monetization, individuals and industries can unlock the immense potential of creative capital, contributing not only to personal wealth but also to the advancement of society as a whole. In the nexus of creativity, commerce, and intellectual property lies the promise of a more innovative, prosperous, and knowledge-driven future.

CHAPTER 16: THE RISE OF THE SOLOPRENEUR: BUILDING PERSONAL BRANDS

Introduction: In the modern entrepreneurial landscape, the concept of success has evolved beyond traditional career paths. The "Rise of the Solopreneur" encapsulates the phenomenon of individuals pursuing their passions and entrepreneurial dreams independently. These solopreneurs leverage their skills, expertise, and personal brand to create businesses that reflect their unique identities and values. This exploration delves into the intricacies of the solopreneurial journey, emphasizing the strategic importance of building personal brands, the role of digital platforms, the impact on traditional employment, and the dynamic relationship between entrepreneurship and self-expression.

Understanding the Solopreneurial Phenomenon: Solopreneurs are individuals who initiate and run their businesses alone, often leveraging their personal skills, expertise, and passions to create value for their clients or customers. This paradigm shift reflects a departure from traditional employment and offers autonomy, flexibility, and the opportunity to align work with personal values.

The Importance of Personal Branding:

1. **Identity and Differentiation:** Personal branding allows solopreneurs to showcase their unique identities, values, and expertise, differentiating them from competitors.

2. **Trust and Credibility:** A strong personal brand fosters trust and credibility among clients, as a well-established reputation can attract loyal customers.

3. **Connection and Authenticity:** Personal brands create a

sense of authenticity, enabling solopreneurs to connect with their audience on a deeper level.

Leveraging Digital Platforms:

1. **Social Media:** Platforms like Instagram, LinkedIn, and Twitter allow solopreneurs to showcase their work, share insights, and engage with their audience.

2. **Blogging and Content Creation:** Blogging and content creation establish expertise and provide valuable information, attracting a dedicated following.

3. **Online Marketplaces:** E-commerce platforms enable solopreneurs to sell products or services online, reaching a global audience without the need for physical storefronts.

Impact on Traditional Employment:

1. **Flexible Work Models:** The solopreneurial trend challenges traditional employment models, emphasizing flexibility, work-life balance, and self-determination.

2. **Gig Economy Integration:** The rise of solopreneurship aligns with the gig economy, where individuals can take on multiple projects and clients.

3. **Economic Contribution:** Solopreneurs contribute to economic growth by creating jobs for themselves and potentially hiring contractors or collaborators.

The Intersection of Entrepreneurship and Self-Expression:

1. **Passion-Driven Ventures:** Solopreneurs often build businesses around their passions, enabling them to pursue work that resonates with their interests.

2. **Personal Fulfillment:** The alignment between entrepreneurship and personal expression fosters a sense of purpose and fulfillment in solopreneurs' work.

Challenges and Considerations:

1. **Time Management:** Balancing various roles—entrepreneur, marketer, content creator—can lead to time management challenges.

2. **Income Stability:** Income may fluctuate for solopreneurs, especially in the early stages. Financial planning and diversification are essential.

3. **Isolation:** Solopreneurs might experience isolation due to the absence of coworkers. Networking and community engagement can mitigate this.

Conclusion: The Rise of the Solopreneur signifies a profound shift in the entrepreneurial landscape—one that celebrates individuality, creativity, and the pursuit of personal passions. As solopreneurs build their businesses, the art of personal branding emerges as a strategic tool, enabling them to differentiate, connect with audiences, and build credibility. Leveraging digital platforms empowers solopreneurs to reach a global audience while impacting traditional employment models and contributing to economic growth. At the heart of this movement lies the fusion of entrepreneurship and self-expression, allowing individuals to find purpose and fulfillment in their work. While challenges exist, the solopreneurial journey embodies the spirit of autonomy, creativity, and innovation that defines the contemporary entrepreneurial spirit.

CHAPTER 17: E-COMMERCE EMPIRES: FROM STARTUP TO SEVEN FIGURES

Introduction: In the rapidly evolving digital landscape, the rise of e-commerce empires stands as a testament to the transformative power of technology and entrepreneurship. "E-commerce Empires: From Startup to Seven Figures" encapsulates the journey of entrepreneurs who have harnessed the potential of online platforms to build lucrative businesses, starting from humble beginnings and scaling to achieve impressive seven-figure revenues. This exploration delves into the intricate layers of the e-commerce journey, encompassing the phases of ideation, establishment, growth strategies, customer engagement, operational efficiency, and the key factors that contribute to the success of these modern business dynasties.

Embarking on the E-commerce Journey:

1. **Idea Generation:** E-commerce empires often begin with a unique product idea, a gap in the market, or a new way to deliver value to customers in the digital sphere.

2. **Market Research:** Thorough market research is vital to identify the target audience, understand their preferences, and assess competition and demand.

Establishment and Early Growth:

1. **Platform Selection:** Entrepreneurs choose between setting up standalone e-commerce websites, utilizing established marketplaces like Amazon and eBay, or a combination of both.

2. **Branding and Positioning:** Building a strong brand identity and positioning ensures differentiation in a competitive market and establishes credibility.

3. **Initial Investments:** Launching an e-commerce

business requires investments in product sourcing, website development, marketing, and initial inventory.

Scaling Strategies:

1. **Diversified Product Lines:** Expanding the product range attracts a broader customer base and increases sales opportunities.

2. **Marketing and Promotion:** Effective digital marketing strategies encompass SEO, content marketing, social media, influencer collaborations, and paid advertising.

3. **Customer Acquisition and Retention:** Building a loyal customer base involves personalized customer experiences, exceptional service, and loyalty programs.

Operational Excellence:

1. **Supply Chain Management:** Streamlining inventory management, logistics, and fulfillment processes ensures timely deliveries and minimizes disruptions.

2. **Customer Service:** Responsive and efficient customer support enhances customer satisfaction and strengthens brand loyalty.

3. **Data Analytics:** Utilizing data analytics helps in understanding customer behavior, optimizing marketing strategies, and identifying growth opportunities.

The Seven-Figure Milestone:

1. **Continuous Innovation:** The journey from startup to seven figures requires ongoing innovation to stay relevant, offer new products, and adapt to market trends.

2. **Strategic Partnerships:** Collaborations with other businesses, influencers, or complementary brands can expand reach and boost sales.

Challenges and Lessons Learned:

1. **Competition:** E-commerce landscapes are often saturated, requiring consistent effort to stand out and offer unique value.

2. **Adaptation:** Being open to pivoting strategies, products, or marketing approaches based on market feedback is crucial for growth.

3. **Scaling Challenges:** Rapid growth may strain resources, necessitating careful planning and investment in infrastructure.

Conclusion: The journey from e-commerce startup to achieving seven-figure revenues is a testament to the power of innovation, resilience, and strategic thinking. E-commerce empires embody the potential of technology and entrepreneurship to shape modern commerce, disrupt traditional business models, and connect businesses directly with customers. This evolution illustrates that with a compelling product, robust strategies, customer-centric approaches, and a commitment to continuous growth, entrepreneurs can leverage the digital realm to create impactful businesses that not only generate substantial revenue but also contribute to the dynamic and ever-changing landscape of the e-commerce ecosystem.

CHAPTER 18: REAL ESTATE REINVENTED: PROPERTY AS A PATH TO PROSPERITY

Introduction: The realm of real estate has undergone a profound transformation, evolving beyond its conventional role as shelter and investment to become a dynamic avenue for achieving prosperity. "Real Estate Reinvented: Property as a Path to Prosperity" captures the essence of this paradigm shift, wherein real estate is seen as a multifaceted vehicle that not only offers physical shelter and financial growth but also serves as a canvas for innovation, sustainability, and community development. This exploration delves deep into the reimagining of real estate, highlighting its role in wealth creation, the fusion of technology and sustainability, changing homeownership dynamics, and the broader implications for individuals and societies.

Real Estate's Role in Wealth Creation:

1. **Investment Potential:** Real estate offers the potential for capital appreciation over time, making it a favored avenue for building wealth.

2. **Rental Income:** Rental properties generate consistent income streams, offering financial stability and passive earnings for investors.

3. **Portfolio Diversification:** Real estate diversifies investment portfolios, reducing risk and providing stability during economic fluctuations.

Technology and Innovation:

1. **Smart Homes:** The integration of technology enables smart homes with automated systems for security, energy efficiency, and convenience.

2. **Proptech Solutions:** PropTech innovations encompass

digital property management, virtual tours, online property auctions, and data-driven investment analysis.

Sustainability and Green Real Estate:

1. **Energy Efficiency:** Sustainable buildings reduce energy consumption and lower operational costs, attracting environmentally conscious buyers and tenants.

2. **Green Infrastructure:** Incorporating green roofs, solar panels, and eco-friendly materials enhances property value and contributes to sustainability goals.

Changing Homeownership Dynamics:

1. **Co-living and Co-working Spaces:** The rise of co-living and co-working spaces reflects changing lifestyle preferences and the need for flexible, community-oriented living arrangements.

2. **Renting vs. Owning:** Shifting attitudes towards homeownership, driven by financial considerations and changing lifestyles, have elevated the appeal of renting.

Community and Social Impact:

1. **Mixed-Use Developments:** Combining residential, commercial, and recreational spaces fosters vibrant communities that promote convenience and social interactions.

2. **Affordable Housing:** Innovations in affordable housing design and financing aim to address the growing demand for accessible housing options.

Challenges and Considerations:

1. **Affordability:** Rising property prices in urban areas can limit access to homeownership and lead to social inequalities.

2. **Regulatory Frameworks:** Real estate operations are governed by complex regulations that impact property development, investment, and management.

3. **Sustainability Implementation:** Incorporating sustainable practices into real estate requires initial investments and a commitment to long-term goals.

Implications for Individuals and Societies:

1. **Economic Growth:** Real estate development contributes to economic growth by creating jobs, attracting investments, and driving demand for related industries.

2. **Urban Planning:** Innovative real estate projects influence urban planning, transforming cities into sustainable, efficient, and community-focused spaces.

3. **Wealth Distribution:** Real estate can contribute to wealth accumulation, but careful planning is required to ensure equitable access and benefits for all segments of society.

Conclusion: "Real Estate Reinvented: Property as a Path to Prosperity" portrays real estate as a canvas for creativity, innovation, and community-building, transcending its traditional role. As technological advancements, sustainability imperatives, and changing lifestyles reshape the way we view and utilize property, the dynamic relationship between real estate and prosperity takes center stage. By embracing technological advancements, sustainability practices, and innovative community-oriented designs, individuals, businesses, and societies can leverage the power of real estate to create a prosperous future that not only generates financial growth but also contributes to the well-being, sustainability, and vibrancy of our urban landscapes.

CHAPTER 19: THE MIND-BENDING POTENTIAL OF BLOCKCHAIN AND CRYPTOCURRENCIES

Introduction: In the digital age, the intersection of technology and finance has given rise to a revolutionary phenomenon: blockchain technology and cryptocurrencies. "The Mind-Bending Potential of Blockchain and Cryptocurrencies" encapsulates the profound impact of these innovations on our understanding of financial systems, data security, decentralization, and the potential to reshape various industries. This exploration delves deep into the intricacies of blockchain, the groundbreaking concept of cryptocurrencies, their transformative potential, challenges, implications for industries, and the future of a decentralized global economy.

Understanding Blockchain:

1. **Decentralization:** Blockchain operates on a decentralized ledger, distributing data across a network of computers, ensuring transparency, security, and immutability.

2. **Cryptographic Security:** Blockchain employs cryptographic techniques to secure data and transactions, reducing the risk of unauthorized access and fraud.

3. **Smart Contracts:** These self-executing contracts automate and validate agreements, eliminating intermediaries and enhancing efficiency.

Cryptocurrencies:

1. **Decentralized Digital Assets:** Cryptocurrencies are digital assets that use cryptography for secure transactions and operate independently of central banks

or governments.

2. **Bitcoin:** Bitcoin, the first cryptocurrency, introduced the concept of digital scarcity and laid the foundation for the entire cryptocurrency ecosystem.

3. **Ethereum:** Ethereum expanded on Bitcoin's capabilities by introducing smart contracts and enabling the creation of decentralized applications (DApps).

Transformative Potential:

1. **Financial Inclusion:** Cryptocurrencies provide access to financial services for the unbanked and underbanked populations worldwide.

2. **Cross-Border Transactions:** Cryptocurrencies facilitate borderless transactions, eliminating the need for currency exchange and traditional intermediaries.

3. **Digital Ownership:** Blockchain enables the tokenization of assets like real estate and art, allowing fractional ownership and enhanced liquidity.

Challenges and Concerns:

1. **Regulatory Uncertainty:** The regulatory landscape for cryptocurrencies varies worldwide, posing challenges for adoption and growth.

2. **Volatility:** The highly volatile nature of cryptocurrency prices can impact their use as a stable medium of exchange or store of value.

3. **Security Concerns:** While blockchain offers robust security, the technology is not immune to cyberattacks and vulnerabilities.

Implications for Industries:

1. **Finance and Banking:** Cryptocurrencies challenge traditional banking models, potentially reducing fees, increasing efficiency, and enhancing financial services accessibility.

2. **Supply Chain Management:** Blockchain ensures transparency and traceability in supply chains, combating counterfeiting and improving accountability.

3. **Healthcare:** Secure data sharing through blockchain can improve patient data management, medical records security, and streamline clinical trials.

4. **Digital Identity:** Blockchain-based digital identity solutions can empower individuals to control their data and simplify identity verification.

The Path Forward:

1. **Mainstream Adoption:** Increasing acceptance of cryptocurrencies by governments, institutions, and consumers may lead to widespread adoption.

2. **Interoperability:** The development of blockchain interoperability solutions can enhance the compatibility of different blockchain networks.

3. **Environmental Impact:** The energy consumption of some blockchain networks raises concerns; innovations like proof-of-stake aim to address this.

Conclusion: "The Mind-Bending Potential of Blockchain and Cryptocurrencies" represents a transformative journey that transcends financial systems, redefines ownership, and challenges traditional paradigms. As blockchain technology and cryptocurrencies continue to evolve, they stand as beacons of innovation, offering a glimpse into a decentralized and digitized future. This journey, while fraught with challenges and uncertainties, holds the potential to democratize financial systems, enhance security, and revolutionize industries, reshaping the way we transact, interact, and collaborate in an increasingly digital world.

CHAPTER 20: HEALTH AND WEALTH FUSION: INVESTING IN WELLNESS VENTURES

Introduction: In the modern age, the convergence of health and wealth has emerged as a powerful paradigm, where investing in wellness ventures holds the promise of not only improving physical and mental well-being but also generating financial prosperity. "Health and Wealth Fusion: Investing in Wellness Ventures" encapsulates the transformative potential of this intersection, where individuals and businesses recognize that investments in health-focused innovations can yield both personal and financial gains. This exploration delves deep into the intricate landscape of wellness entrepreneurship, the burgeoning health and wellness industry, innovative investment opportunities, the societal impact of well-being initiatives, and the holistic nature of a prosperous future.

The Wellness Revolution:

1. **Wellness Industry Growth:** The wellness sector spans fitness, nutrition, mental health, alternative therapies, and preventive medicine, offering a diverse range of investment avenues.

2. **Consumer Awareness:** Increasing awareness of well-being's impact on overall quality of life has driven demand for health-focused products and services.

Investment Opportunities in Wellness Ventures:

1. **Nutrition and Dietary Supplements:** Investing in companies that offer organic and functional foods, supplements, and personalized nutrition solutions.

2. **Fitness Technology:** Backing fitness tech startups creating wearable devices, fitness apps, and virtual

training platforms.

3. **Mindfulness and Mental Health:** Supporting companies that provide mental health services, meditation apps, and stress management tools.

The Synergy of Health and Wealth:

1. **Long-Term Benefits:** Investing in wellness ventures can lead to long-term savings by promoting preventative health measures and reducing healthcare costs.

2. **Productivity and Performance:** Healthier individuals tend to be more productive and engaged, contributing positively to their professional endeavors.

3. **Holistic Prosperity:** The fusion of health and wealth creates a holistic sense of well-being, enhancing the quality of life on multiple levels.

Societal Implications:

1. **Healthier Communities:** Wellness ventures foster healthier communities, reducing the burden on healthcare systems and enhancing overall societal well-being.

2. **Innovation Ecosystem:** Investing in wellness innovation supports research, development, and adoption of technologies that positively impact health outcomes.

3. **Job Creation:** The growth of the wellness sector creates job opportunities in areas such as fitness, nutrition, healthcare, and technology.

Challenges and Considerations:

1. **Regulatory Compliance:** The wellness industry is subject to regulations that vary globally, requiring careful navigation.

2. **Ethical Concerns:** Balancing profit motives with ethical considerations, especially in healthcare-related

ventures, is crucial.

3. **Market Saturation:** As the wellness industry expands, competition increases, necessitating unique value propositions for sustainable success.

The Role of Technology:

1. **Digital Health Platforms:** Technology enables remote health monitoring, telehealth services, and access to personalized health data.

2. **Data Analytics:** Analyzing health data can identify trends, optimize wellness strategies, and enhance user experiences.

Investor Considerations:

1. **Due Diligence:** Thorough research is essential to assess the viability, sustainability, and growth potential of wellness ventures.

2. **Diversification:** A well-rounded portfolio includes diverse investments across various segments of the wellness industry.

Conclusion: The fusion of health and wealth embodies a progressive vision where investments not only create financial gains but also contribute to personal well-being, community health, and societal advancement. "Health and Wealth Fusion: Investing in Wellness Ventures" represents a transformative journey, where entrepreneurs and investors alike recognize the potential of well-being-focused innovations to create a prosperous and fulfilling future. By aligning financial success with the promotion of health and wellness, individuals, businesses, and societies have the opportunity to redefine prosperity, shifting from a narrow definition based solely on financial wealth to a holistic concept that encompasses physical vitality, mental well-being, and a sustainable and prosperous future for all.

CHAPTER 21: CULTURAL TRENDS AND MARKET DOMINATION: CAPITALIZING ON SHIFTS

Introduction: In the dynamic global landscape, cultural trends serve as powerful indicators of societal shifts and preferences. Capitalizing on these cultural trends enables businesses to align their strategies with evolving consumer demands, thereby achieving market domination. "Cultural Trends and Market Domination" delves into the profound impact of cultural shifts on industries, the art of recognizing and adapting to emerging trends, strategies for market dominance, challenges, and the symbiotic relationship between businesses and evolving cultural landscapes.

Cultural Trends as Catalysts:

1. **Reflecting Society:** Cultural trends mirror changing values, behaviors, and aspirations of society, making them crucial signals for businesses to understand.

2. **Consumer Preferences:** Businesses that tap into cultural trends gain insights into what resonates with consumers, enhancing their ability to create relevant offerings.

Adapting to Emerging Trends:

1. **Consumer-Centric Approach:** Understanding cultural shifts helps businesses tailor products, services, and messaging to match evolving consumer preferences.

2. **Innovation and Creativity:** Cultural trends inspire innovative solutions that cater to new demands and create competitive differentiators.

Strategies for Market Domination:

1. **Early Adoption:** Recognizing cultural trends early

allows businesses to position themselves as pioneers and market leaders.

2. **Agile Business Models:** Businesses that can pivot quickly to align with emerging trends gain a competitive advantage.

3. **Authentic Branding:** Authenticity resonates with consumers drawn to brands that genuinely align with their values and cultural sensibilities.

Cultural Trends Across Industries:

1. **Fashion and Beauty:** The fashion and beauty industry thrives on cultural shifts, responding to changing aesthetics, sustainability concerns, and inclusivity.

2. **Food and Beverage:** Culinary trends reflect changing dietary preferences, cultural influences, and sustainability considerations.

3. **Entertainment and Media:** Cultural trends influence content creation, leading to the production of media that resonates with diverse audiences.

Challenges and Considerations:

1. **Cultural Sensitivity:** Adapting to cultural trends requires sensitivity to avoid cultural appropriation or misinterpretation.

2. **Rapid Change:** Cultural trends evolve quickly; businesses must be agile to respond effectively and maintain relevance.

3. **Balancing Tradition and Innovation:** Businesses must strike a balance between embracing cultural shifts and preserving core values.

The Cultural-Brand Nexus:

1. **Mutual Influence:** Brands impact cultural trends by shaping societal perceptions, while cultural shifts influence brand strategies.

2. **Social Responsibility:** Brands that champion social causes aligned with cultural trends can earn trust and loyalty from consumers.

Globalization and Localization:

1. **Cultural Universality:** Some cultural trends have a global appeal, enabling businesses to connect with diverse audiences worldwide.

2. **Local Adaptation:** Navigating cultural trends requires understanding local nuances to tailor offerings to specific markets.

Conclusion: "Cultural Trends and Market Domination" showcases the intricate dance between evolving cultural landscapes and business strategies. By harnessing the power of cultural trends, businesses can anticipate consumer desires, innovate, and create resonant offerings that lead to market dominance. This synergy between culture and commerce underscores the importance of staying attuned to societal shifts, embracing authenticity, and fostering a deep understanding of consumer preferences. In a world shaped by constant change, the harmonious fusion of cultural trends and business strategies paves the way for enduring market dominance and sustainable success.

CHAPTER 22: THE INVESTOR'S ARSENAL: TOOLS FOR ANALYZING MODERN MARKETS

Introduction: In the fast-paced and complex world of modern finance, successful investing requires more than just intuition—it demands a comprehensive understanding of the markets, advanced analytical tools, and data-driven insights. "The Investor's Arsenal: Tools for Analyzing Modern Markets" encapsulates the array of sophisticated tools and methodologies that investors wield to navigate volatile markets, make informed decisions, manage risks, and uncover opportunities. This exploration delves deep into the multifaceted landscape of modern market analysis, encompassing fundamental analysis, technical analysis, quantitative methods, artificial intelligence, big data analytics, and the integration of these tools to create a robust investor's arsenal.

Fundamental Analysis:

1. **Company Financials:** Evaluating a company's financial statements to assess its profitability, growth prospects, and financial health.

2. **Market Research:** Analyzing industry trends, competitive landscape, and market dynamics to identify growth potential and challenges.

3. **Valuation Models:** Utilizing techniques like discounted cash flow (DCF) analysis and price-to-earnings (P/E) ratios to determine a company's intrinsic value.

Technical Analysis:

1. **Price Patterns:** Identifying chart patterns, such as head and shoulders or double bottoms, to predict future price movements.

2. **Indicators:** Utilizing technical indicators like moving averages, Relative Strength Index (RSI), and Bollinger Bands to gauge market momentum and overbought/oversold conditions.

3. **Candlestick Patterns:** Interpreting candlestick patterns to understand market sentiment and potential reversals.

Quantitative Methods:

1. **Algorithmic Trading:** Developing trading algorithms that execute trades based on predefined rules, leveraging speed and precision.

2. **Statistical Models:** Applying regression analysis, time series analysis, and machine learning algorithms to predict market behavior.

3. **Portfolio Optimization:** Utilizing techniques like the Markowitz mean-variance optimization to create diversified portfolios with optimal risk-return profiles.

Artificial Intelligence and Big Data Analytics:

1. **Machine Learning:** Employing machine learning algorithms to identify patterns, make predictions, and uncover hidden correlations in vast datasets.

2. **Sentiment Analysis:** Analyzing social media, news sentiment, and market sentiment to gauge investor sentiment and potential market reactions.

3. **Predictive Analytics:** Using historical data and predictive models to forecast market trends, price movements, and economic indicators.

Integrated Analysis:

1. **Holistic Approach:** Integrating fundamental analysis, technical analysis, and quantitative methods to validate investment decisions.

2. **Scenario Analysis:** Evaluating different scenarios

and stress-testing portfolios to understand potential outcomes in various market conditions.

Challenges and Considerations:

1. **Data Quality:** The accuracy and quality of data used in analysis are crucial for making informed decisions.

2. **Overfitting:** Applying complex models without considering the risk of overfitting to historical data, leading to inaccurate predictions.

3. **Market Volatility:** Rapid market changes can challenge the accuracy of predictions and require adaptive strategies.

Conclusion: "The Investor's Arsenal: Tools for Analyzing Modern Markets" underscores the importance of leveraging a diverse range of tools and methodologies to thrive in today's intricate financial landscape. Successful investors employ a strategic blend of fundamental analysis, technical analysis, quantitative methods, artificial intelligence, and big data analytics to gain a comprehensive understanding of markets and make well-informed decisions. By harnessing the power of these tools, investors can navigate uncertainty, manage risks, seize opportunities, and achieve their financial goals in the ever-evolving world of modern finance.

CHAPTER 23: FROM EMPLOYEE TO ENTREPRENEUR: UNLEASHING HIDDEN POTENTIAL

Introduction: The transition from employee to entrepreneur represents a significant paradigm shift, where individuals step away from traditional employment to embark on a journey of self-discovery, innovation, and realizing their hidden potential. "From Employee to Entrepreneur: Unleashing Hidden Potential" encapsulates the transformative process of transitioning from the structured confines of employment to the dynamic world of entrepreneurship. This exploration delves deep into the multifaceted aspects of this journey, encompassing self-awareness, mindset shifts, identifying opportunities, risk management, skills cultivation, challenges, and the ultimate reward of self-actualization and business success.

The Call to Entrepreneurship:

1. **Desire for Autonomy:** The pursuit of greater independence, decision-making control, and the ability to shape one's destiny fuels the entrepreneurial drive.

2. **Passion and Purpose:** Entrepreneurs often seek to align their work with their passions, channeling their energy into ventures that resonate with their values.

Mindset Transformation:

1. **Risk Tolerance:** Embracing calculated risks and overcoming the fear of failure are crucial components of the entrepreneurial mindset.

2. **Adaptability:** Entrepreneurs must develop the ability to pivot and adapt swiftly in response to changing market dynamics.

3. **Growth Mindset:** Cultivating a growth mindset fosters a

willingness to learn, iterate, and continuously improve in the face of challenges.

Identifying Opportunities:

1. **Market Research:** Conducting thorough market research helps identify unmet needs, gaps, and opportunities for innovative solutions.

2. **Problem Solving:** Entrepreneurs address real-world problems and create value by developing products or services that address specific pain points.

Skills Development:

1. **Multifaceted Skill Set:** Entrepreneurs wear many hats, requiring skills in sales, marketing, finance, operations, and more.

2. **Continuous Learning:** Adapting to the evolving business landscape necessitates ongoing learning and skill enhancement.

Risk Management:

1. **Calculated Ventures:** Entrepreneurs balance risk-taking with strategic planning to mitigate potential pitfalls.

2. **Financial Planning:** Effective financial management ensures sustainability and growth, reducing the impact of financial uncertainties.

Challenges and Resilience:

1. **Uncertainty:** The entrepreneurial journey is marked by uncertainties, requiring resilience, perseverance, and adaptability.

2. **Time Management:** Balancing various responsibilities and tasks can challenge entrepreneurs' time management skills.

3. **Resource Constraints:** Limited financial resources and the need to wear multiple hats demand resourcefulness.

Rewards of Entrepreneurship:

1. **Self-Actualization:** Entrepreneurship provides a platform for self-expression, creativity, and realizing one's full potential.

2. **Financial Independence:** Successful ventures can lead to financial rewards and long-term prosperity.

3. **Impact:** Entrepreneurs contribute to societal progress by creating jobs, driving innovation, and addressing unmet needs.

Conclusion: "From Employee to Entrepreneur: Unleashing Hidden Potential" represents a transformative journey of self-discovery, innovation, and empowerment. As individuals transition from employee roles to entrepreneurial endeavors, they embark on a path of continuous growth, learning, and adaptation. This journey requires a shift in mindset, the cultivation of diverse skills, risk management, and the resilience to overcome challenges. Ultimately, the rewards of entrepreneurship go beyond financial gain, offering individuals the chance to unleash their hidden potential, create meaningful impact, and redefine success on their terms. By embracing the entrepreneurial spirit and embarking on this empowering journey, individuals have the opportunity to shape their destinies, contribute to society, and leave a lasting legacy of innovation and achievement.

CHAPTER 24: PHILANTHROPY AND IMPACT: THE ALTRUISTIC FACE OF WEALTH

Introduction: Wealth, when harnessed with a philanthropic spirit, transcends its material significance and becomes a powerful force for positive change. "Philanthropy and Impact: The Altruistic Face of Wealth" delves into the profound realm where individuals and entities, fueled by their financial success, channel their resources, time, and expertise to create enduring social impact. This exploration delves deep into the multifaceted landscape of philanthropy, encompassing the motivations, strategies, societal transformations, global challenges, innovative approaches, and the potential to catalyze a more equitable and compassionate world.

The Motivations Behind Philanthropy:

1. **Social Responsibility:** Individuals recognize their privilege and feel a moral obligation to give back and address societal inequalities.

2. **Legacy Building:** Philanthropy allows individuals to leave a lasting legacy, making a meaningful mark on the world.

3. **Personal Fulfillment:** Giving provides a sense of purpose, happiness, and fulfillment that transcends material wealth.

Strategies for Effective Philanthropy:

1. **Strategic Grantmaking:** Targeted funding of projects aligned with personal values and social impact goals.

2. **Capacity Building:** Investing in organizational infrastructure to enhance nonprofits' efficiency and effectiveness.

3. **Collaborative Approaches:** Partnerships with other donors, NGOs, and governments amplify philanthropic impact.

Philanthropic Impact on Society:

1. **Education:** Funding educational initiatives expands access to quality education, empowering individuals and fostering economic development.

2. **Healthcare:** Philanthropy bolsters healthcare systems, improving access to medical care, research, and disease prevention.

3. **Poverty Alleviation:** Providing resources, vocational training, and microfinance empowers marginalized communities to escape poverty.

Tackling Global Challenges:

1. **Climate Change:** Philanthropy supports initiatives addressing environmental challenges and advancing sustainability.

2. **Global Health Crises:** Philanthropic efforts combat pandemics and improve global healthcare infrastructure.

3. **Social Injustice:** Philanthropy fights systemic discrimination, advancing social justice and equality.

Innovative Philanthropic Approaches:

1. **Impact Investing:** Channeling investments into projects that generate social and environmental impact alongside financial returns.

2. **Technology for Good:** Leveraging technology to solve social issues, from digital education to healthcare access.

3. **Catalytic Philanthropy:** Funding initiatives that serve as catalysts for broader systemic change.

Challenges and Considerations:

1. **Effective Allocation:** Maximizing impact requires strategic allocation of resources and measuring outcomes.

2. **Sustainability:** Philanthropy must address long-term sustainability, ensuring initiatives continue to thrive.

3. **Cultural Sensitivity:** Philanthropic efforts must be culturally respectful and tailored to local contexts.

The Power of Collective Giving:

1. **Giving Circles:** Groups of individuals pool resources to collectively make a larger impact.

2. **Corporate Philanthropy:** Corporations leverage resources and expertise for social causes, aligning with corporate social responsibility.

Creating Lasting Change:

1. **Social Transformation:** Philanthropy drives systemic change by addressing root causes and catalyzing broad impact.

2. **Inspiring Others:** Philanthropic efforts encourage others to give, creating a ripple effect of generosity.

Conclusion: "Philanthropy and Impact: The Altruistic Face of Wealth" unveils the transformative potential of wealth when guided by altruism and a commitment to making the world a better place. Philanthropy transcends charity, becoming a powerful catalyst for social progress, equity, and positive change. As individuals, organizations, and even corporations engage in philanthropic endeavors, they shape a future marked by compassion, empowerment, and social transformation. This journey represents a convergence of wealth, purpose, and humanity, where the act of giving extends far beyond the material realm to ignite a brighter and more compassionate world for generations to come.

CHAPTER 25: FAMILY OFFICE STRATEGIES: MANAGING MULTIGENERATIONAL WEALTH

Introduction: Multigenerational wealth presents a unique set of challenges and opportunities that require strategic and tailored management. "Family Office Strategies: Managing Multigenerational Wealth" delves into the intricacies of preserving, growing, and distributing wealth across multiple generations. This exploration uncovers the multifaceted world of family offices, encompassing governance, succession planning, investment strategies, philanthropy, education, communication, and the delicate balance of ensuring financial prosperity while maintaining family cohesion.

Family Office Evolution:

1. **Origins:** Family offices originated as a way to manage the financial affairs of wealthy families, evolving into comprehensive platforms for holistic wealth management.

2. **Wealth Preservation:** The primary goal is to ensure the longevity of wealth through strategic planning and prudent decision-making.

Governance and Family Dynamics:

1. **Family Constitution:** Establishing a formal document that outlines family values, goals, and decision-making processes.

2. **Communication:** Open and transparent communication fosters trust, minimizes conflicts, and strengthens family bonds.

3. **Conflict Resolution:** Addressing conflicts promptly and respectfully prevents disputes from jeopardizing family

unity and wealth management.

Succession Planning:

1. **Next-Generation Development:** Preparing the younger generation through education, mentoring, and leadership training.

2. **Smooth Transition:** Ensuring a seamless transition of leadership, roles, and responsibilities across generations.

Investment Strategies:

1. **Diversification:** Developing a diversified investment portfolio to mitigate risks and capitalize on various opportunities.

2. **Long-Term Perspective:** Aligning investments with the family's long-term objectives and risk tolerance.

Philanthropic Endeavors:

1. **Social Responsibility:** Philanthropy allows families to contribute positively to society while transmitting values to younger generations.

2. **Impactful Giving:** Identifying strategic causes that align with family values and maximizing the impact of philanthropic efforts.

Educational Initiatives:

1. **Financial Literacy:** Equipping family members with the knowledge and skills needed to make informed financial decisions.

2. **Entrepreneurial Education:** Supporting entrepreneurship and innovation within the family to foster sustainable growth.

Risk Management:

1. **Estate Planning:** Developing comprehensive estate plans to minimize taxes, ensure smooth wealth transfer,

and safeguard assets.

2. **Insurance:** Implementing risk management strategies, including life insurance and liability coverage, to protect family wealth.

Technology and Innovation:

1. **Digital Transformation:** Embracing technology to streamline operations, enhance reporting, and improve decision-making.

2. **Investment Analytics:** Utilizing data analytics to make informed investment decisions and monitor performance.

Challenges and Considerations:

1. **Family Dynamics:** Balancing differing opinions, aspirations, and goals among family members.

2. **Maintaining Cohesion:** Ensuring that wealth management decisions do not compromise family relationships.

3. **Market Volatility:** Navigating market fluctuations and economic uncertainties while preserving wealth.

Legacy and Impact:

1. **Preserving Values:** Family offices cultivate a legacy of values, culture, and social responsibility across generations.

2. **Community Impact:** Leveraging wealth to create positive societal change and contribute to the betterment of communities.

Conclusion: "Family Office Strategies: Managing Multigenerational Wealth" represents a holistic approach to preserving wealth and family unity through strategic planning, transparent communication, and long-term vision. As families navigate the complexities of multigenerational wealth management, they create a legacy that extends beyond financial prosperity, encompassing shared values, education, philanthropy, and societal impact. This journey exemplifies the fusion of financial acumen, interpersonal skills, and a commitment to ensuring the well-being of both present and future generations, setting the stage for enduring prosperity and meaningful contributions to society.

CHAPTER 26: ART AND AESTHETICS AS INVESTMENT: THE CREATIVE ECONOMY

Introduction: The intersection of art and investment has given rise to the creative economy, a realm where art and aesthetics hold the potential for both financial returns and cultural enrichment. "Art and Aesthetics as Investment: The Creative Economy" delves into the captivating world where artistic expression and economic value converge. This exploration unveils the multifaceted dynamics of investing in art, encompassing market trends, valuation methodologies, the significance of cultural capital, risk management, fostering creativity, and the profound impact of the creative economy on societies and individuals.

The Creative Economy Unveiled:

1. **Diverse Sectors:** The creative economy extends beyond traditional art to include design, fashion, media, architecture, and entertainment.

2. **Cultural Capital:** Art and creativity contribute to a nation's cultural identity, fostering innovation and societal progress.

Art as an Investment:

1. **Historical Appreciation:** The value of art has historically appreciated, making it an attractive alternative investment.

2. **Tangible and Intangible Returns:** Art investment offers financial gains alongside the intangible satisfaction of owning a piece of cultural history.

Market Trends and Valuation:

1. **Art Market Dynamics:** The art market experiences cyclical trends driven by factors such as artist recognition, collector demand, and economic

conditions.

2. **Valuation Complexities:** Determining the value of art involves assessing provenance, rarity, artist reputation, and market demand.

Risk and Risk Management:

1. **Volatility:** The art market can be volatile due to subjective value perceptions, market sentiment, and changes in taste.

2. **Expertise and Due Diligence:** In-depth research, expert guidance, and thorough provenance verification are essential for minimizing risks.

Cultural Capital and Societal Impact:

1. **Artistic Enrichment:** Investing in art supports artists and cultural initiatives, enriching societies and preserving heritage.

2. **Tourism and Cultural Exchange:** The creative economy fosters cultural tourism, promoting global understanding and appreciation.

Supporting Creativity and Innovation:

1. **Artist Empowerment:** Art investment provides financial support and exposure for emerging artists, fostering innovation.

2. **Cross-Pollination:** Collaboration between artists, industries, and disciplines leads to innovative solutions and fresh perspectives.

Art Investment Strategies:

1. **Diversification:** Building a diverse art portfolio across genres, mediums, and artists reduces risk.

2. **Long-Term Perspective:** Art investment often requires a patient approach, allowing time for appreciation.

Challenges and Considerations:

1. **Authenticity:** Ensuring the authenticity of artworks is vital to prevent investment in forgeries.

2. **Liquidity:** Art is not as liquid as traditional investments, requiring careful planning for potential sales.

3. **Market Knowledge:** Staying informed about art market trends and cultural shifts is essential for informed investment decisions.

The Role of Technology:

1. **Digital Art:** Blockchain technology enables secure ownership and trading of digital art.

2. **Virtual Galleries:** Online platforms democratize access to art, expanding the reach of artists and collectors.

Conclusion: "Art and Aesthetics as Investment: The Creative Economy" captures the essence of the creative realm where aesthetics intertwine with investment potential. Art investment offers both financial rewards and cultural enrichment, fostering creativity, innovation, and societal progress. By navigating the intricacies of the art market, valuing cultural capital, and fostering creativity, individuals and societies can experience the transformative power of the creative economy. This journey transcends financial gains, embracing the beauty of artistic expression, cultural preservation, and the enduring impact of art on both individuals and the world at large.

CHAPTER 27: THE NEUROBIOLOGY OF SUCCESS: HACKING PRODUCTIVITY AND FOCUS

Introduction: Achieving success in the modern world demands more than just hard work—it requires an understanding of the intricate workings of the human brain. "The Neurobiology of Success: Hacking Productivity and Focus" delves into the fascinating realm of neuroscience, uncovering the hidden mechanisms that govern productivity, focus, and peak performance. This exploration dives deep into the neuroscience of success, encompassing brain functions, neural pathways, cognitive strategies, mindfulness, brain-boosting practices, and the potential to unlock unparalleled levels of achievement and fulfillment.

Understanding Brain Functions:

1. **Neural Networks:** The brain operates through complex networks of neurons that transmit information and facilitate communication.

2. **Neuroplasticity:** The brain's ability to reorganize itself through learning and experience, facilitating adaptability and skill acquisition.

Cognitive Processes for Success:

1. **Executive Functioning:** Cognitive processes such as planning, decision-making, and impulse control play a crucial role in achieving goals.

2. **Working Memory:** The brain's capacity to hold and manipulate information influences problem-solving and creative thinking.

Neural Pathways of Focus and Productivity:

1. **Prefrontal Cortex:** This region governs attention, focus,

and cognitive control, key for maintaining productivity.

2. **Default Mode Network:** Active during rest, it contributes to creative insights, problem-solving, and consolidating information.

Mindfulness and Cognitive Enhancement:

1. **Mindfulness Practices:** Techniques like meditation and mindfulness enhance attention, stress management, and cognitive clarity.

2. **Neurofeedback:** Training the brain to regulate its own activity improves self-awareness and cognitive functioning.

Dopamine and Motivation:

1. **Dopaminergic System:** Dopamine influences motivation, reward, and pleasure, driving goal-oriented behavior.

2. **Reward Pathway Activation:** Setting and achieving goals trigger dopamine release, reinforcing positive behaviors.

Sleep and Brain Health:

1. **Sleep's Role:** Adequate sleep supports cognitive functions, memory consolidation, and overall brain health.

2. **Circadian Rhythms:** Aligning activities with the body's natural rhythm optimizes focus and productivity.

Boosting Brain Performance:

1. **Nutrition and Brain Health:** A balanced diet rich in antioxidants, omega-3 fatty acids, and brain-boosting nutrients supports cognitive function.

2. **Physical Exercise:** Exercise enhances blood flow, oxygenation, and the release of brain-derived neurotrophic factor (BDNF), which supports brain

growth.

Technological Tools and Brain Enhancement:

1. **Cognitive Training Apps:** Digital platforms offer brain-training exercises targeting memory, attention, and problem-solving.

2. **Neurofeedback Devices:** Wearable devices provide real-time feedback to help users regulate brain activity.

The Role of Dopamine and Rewards:

1. **Goal Setting:** Breaking down goals into smaller milestones triggers dopamine release, promoting motivation.

2. **Intrinsic vs. Extrinsic Rewards:** Intrinsic satisfaction from accomplishing tasks fuels long-term motivation.

Challenges and Strategies:

1. **Digital Distractions:** Managing technology usage to prevent digital distractions and improve focus.

2. **Stress Management:** Stress reduction techniques enhance cognitive resilience and decision-making.

Conclusion: "The Neurobiology of Success: Hacking Productivity and Focus" uncovers the inner workings of the brain, offering insights into achieving peak performance, focus, and productivity. By harnessing knowledge from neuroscience, individuals can optimize cognitive processes, cultivate mindfulness, and make informed lifestyle choices that lead to success. This journey, rooted in the understanding of brain functions, pathways, and strategies, enables individuals to unlock their fullest potential, harness the power of their minds, and create a roadmap to sustained success and fulfillment in an increasingly complex and demanding world.

CHAPTER 28: TAX OPTIMIZATION IN A COMPLEX FINANCIAL LANDSCAPE

Introduction: In a dynamic financial landscape marked by changing regulations, diverse income streams, and intricate investment vehicles, mastering tax optimization has become paramount. "Tax Optimization in a Complex Financial Landscape" delves into the multifaceted world of tax planning, offering insights into strategies for mitigating tax liabilities, preserving wealth, complying with legal frameworks, and achieving long-term financial goals. This exploration delves deep into the intricacies of tax optimization, encompassing tax-efficient investments, estate planning, retirement strategies, international tax considerations, and the profound impact of prudent tax management on overall financial success.

Navigating the Tax Landscape:

1. **Changing Tax Codes:** Evolving tax laws require continuous monitoring and adaptation to maximize benefits.

2. **Income Streams:** Diverse income sources necessitate strategic planning to optimize tax implications.

Tax-Efficient Investment Strategies:

1. **Asset Location:** Allocating investments across taxable and tax-advantaged accounts to minimize tax liability.

2. **Tax-Efficient Funds:** Investing in funds designed to minimize capital gains distributions and taxable income.

Estate Planning and Wealth Transfer:

1. **Estate Tax Planning:** Minimizing estate tax exposure while ensuring efficient wealth transfer to beneficiaries.

2. **Gift and Trust Strategies:** Utilizing trusts, gifts, and charitable giving to optimize wealth transfer and tax benefits.

Retirement Planning and Tax Efficiency:

1. **Tax-Advantaged Accounts:** Maximizing contributions to retirement accounts like IRAs and 401(k)s for long-term growth.

2. **Roth Conversions:** Strategically converting traditional retirement accounts to Roth accounts for tax-free withdrawals in retirement.

International Tax Considerations:

1. **Foreign Income:** Navigating the complexities of reporting and managing taxes on foreign-sourced income.

2. **Tax Treaties:** Leveraging bilateral tax treaties to minimize double taxation for individuals with international financial ties.

Business Ownership and Tax Optimization:

1. **Entity Selection:** Choosing the optimal business structure to minimize both corporate and individual tax liabilities.

2. **Pass-Through Entities:** Utilizing entities like S corporations and partnerships to pass income through to shareholders or partners.

Tax-Efficient Charitable Giving:

1. **Donor-Advised Funds:** Contributing to donor-advised funds to consolidate and strategically manage charitable donations.

2. **Qualified Charitable Distributions:** Using required minimum distributions from retirement accounts for tax-efficient charitable giving.

Complexities and Compliance:

1. **Tax Planning vs. Tax Evasion:** Adhering to ethical tax practices while optimizing tax liabilities within the bounds of the law.

2. **Reporting Requirements:** Ensuring accurate and timely reporting of financial transactions to remain compliant.

Professional Collaboration:

1. **Financial Advisors and CPAs:** Collaborating with professionals to develop comprehensive tax optimization strategies.

2. **Annual Reviews:** Regularly reviewing financial and tax plans to adapt to changing circumstances and regulations.

Conclusion: "Tax Optimization in a Complex Financial Landscape" underscores the critical role of strategic tax planning in preserving wealth, achieving financial goals, and navigating a multifaceted financial world. By employing tax-efficient investment strategies, managing international tax implications, and crafting comprehensive estate and retirement plans, individuals can position themselves for long-term success. This journey through tax optimization, marked by strategic decision-making, collaboration with professionals, and adherence to legal standards, ultimately empowers individuals to navigate complexity, preserve assets, and secure their financial future in an ever-changing tax landscape.

CHAPTER 29: THE PSYCHOLOGY OF CONSUMERISM: TAPPING INTO BUYING BEHAVIOR

Introduction: Consumerism is a defining aspect of modern society, and understanding the psychology behind buying behavior is essential for businesses, marketers, and even individuals. "The Psychology of Consumerism: Tapping into Buying Behavior" delves into the complex web of psychological factors that drive consumer decisions, exploring the cognitive processes, emotional triggers, social influences, and cultural dynamics that shape how and why people make purchases. This exploration delves deep into the realms of motivation, decision-making, branding, advertising, consumer loyalty, and the intricate interplay between psychology and commerce in the modern world.

Cognitive Processes in Consumer Decision-Making:

1. **Perception:** How consumers perceive products, brands, and messages influences their purchasing choices.

2. **Attention and Memory:** Effective marketing captures attention and creates memorable experiences to influence future decisions.

3. **Information Processing:** Consumers seek information, evaluate options, and make decisions based on perceived benefits.

Emotional Triggers and Buying Behavior:

1. **Emotional Branding:** Brands tap into emotions to form connections, often through storytelling and relatable experiences.

2. **Emotional Needs:** Purchases fulfill emotional needs such as status, security, belonging, or self-expression.

Social Influences and Consumer Choices:

1. **Social Proof:** Consumers look to others' behaviors and choices as indicators of what is acceptable or desirable.

2. **Influence of Reference Groups:** Peer groups, families, and communities' impact what products and brands consumers prefer.

Cultural Dynamics and Consumer Behavior:

1. **Cultural Values:** Consumer choices are influenced by cultural norms, values, and societal expectations.

2. **Cultural Symbolism:** Products often carry cultural meanings and associations that influence their desirability.

Branding and Advertising Strategies:

1. **Brand Identity:** Brands create unique personalities that resonate with consumer aspirations and values.

2. **Advertising Appeals:** Emotional appeals, humor, fear, and nostalgia evoke different emotional responses and buying motivations.

Consumer Decision-Making Models:

1. **Cognitive Model:** Consumers make rational decisions based on utility, evaluating benefits and costs.

2. **Emotional Model:** Emotions play a central role in decision-making, with rationality playing a supporting role.

The Role of Scarcity and Urgency:

1. **Scarcity Principle:** Limited availability or time-sensitive offers trigger a fear of missing out (FOMO), influencing purchases.

2. **Urgency Tactics:** Promotions with time constraints create a sense of urgency that encourages immediate action.

Building Consumer Loyalty:

1. **Brand Loyalty:** Consumers stick to familiar brands due to trust, perceived quality, and positive experiences.

2. **Loyalty Programs:** Offering rewards and incentives encourages repeat purchases and fosters long-term relationships.

Consumer Behavior in the Digital Age:

1. **E-Commerce and Personalization:** Online platforms use data to tailor offerings, enhancing consumer experiences.

2. **Social Media Influence:** Influencers and peer endorsements on social media impact buying choices.

Ethics and Sustainability in Consumerism:

1. **Conscious Consumerism:** Consumers consider ethical and environmental factors in their purchasing decisions.

2. **Corporate Social Responsibility:** Brands that align with consumers' values attract loyal customers.

Conclusion: "The Psychology of Consumerism: Tapping into Buying Behavior" unravels the intricate dance between psychology and commerce, shedding light on the myriad factors that drive consumer choices. By understanding the cognitive, emotional, social, and cultural dynamics that influence buying behavior, businesses can craft effective marketing strategies and build meaningful relationships with consumers. This journey through the psychology of consumerism underscores the fusion of human psychology, marketing tactics, and societal trends, shaping the consumer landscape and driving economic activity in a world where perceptions, emotions, and motivations converge in the realm of commerce.

CHAPTER 30: AI AND AUTOMATION: STREAMLINING BUSINESS FOR MAXIMUM GAIN

Introduction: Artificial Intelligence (AI) and automation have emerged as transformative forces reshaping the landscape of business operations. "AI and Automation: Streamlining Business for Maximum Gain" delves into the intricate realm where cutting-edge technologies converge to streamline processes, enhance decision-making, and optimize resource allocation. This exploration uncovers the multifaceted dimensions of AI and automation, encompassing their applications across industries, impacts on job roles, ethical considerations, challenges, benefits, and the profound potential to elevate business efficiency and drive sustainable growth.

Understanding AI and Automation:

1. **AI Definition:** AI refers to the simulation of human intelligence in machines, enabling them to perform tasks that typically require human intelligence.

2. **Automation Definition:** Automation involves using technology to perform tasks with minimal human intervention, reducing manual effort.

Applications Across Industries:

1. **Manufacturing:** Robotics and automation streamline production, enhance precision, and increase output.

2. **Healthcare:** AI aids in medical diagnosis, drug discovery, and personalized treatment plans.

3. **Finance:** Algorithms enable automated trading, fraud detection, and risk assessment.

Enhancing Decision-Making:

1. **Data Analysis:** AI processes vast amounts of data to generate insights that inform strategic decisions.
2. **Predictive Analytics:** Algorithms forecast trends, enabling proactive planning and resource allocation.

Operational Efficiency and Cost Savings:

1. **Process Automation:** Routine tasks, from data entry to customer support, can be automated, reducing human error and saving time.
2. **Resource Optimization:** AI predicts demand, enabling efficient inventory management and production planning.

Impact on Job Roles:

1. **Job Transformation:** While certain tasks become automated, new roles emerge in AI development, maintenance, and oversight.
2. **Reskilling:** Upskilling the workforce prepares employees for roles requiring complex problem-solving and creative thinking.

Ethical Considerations:

1. **Bias and Fairness:** AI systems can perpetuate biases present in training data, necessitating fair algorithms.
2. **Job Displacement:** Automation can lead to job loss, prompting ethical concerns about workers' livelihoods.

Challenges and Overcoming Resistance:

1. **Change Management:** Employees may resist automation due to fear of job loss or unfamiliarity with technology.
2. **Integration Complexities:** Implementing AI and automation requires careful integration with existing systems.

Customer Experience Enhancement:

1. **Personalization:** AI-driven recommendations and chatbots enhance customer interactions and satisfaction.

2. **24/7 Availability:** Automation enables round-the-clock service, enhancing customer convenience.

Benefits of AI and Automation:

1. **Scalability:** Automated processes can scale up or down rapidly based on demand.

2. **Consistency:** Automation ensures tasks are performed consistently, reducing human error.

Innovation and Creativity:

1. **Reducing Mundane Tasks:** Automation frees up human resources for higher-level tasks that require creativity and innovation.

2. **Rapid Development:** AI accelerates product development through predictive modeling and data analysis.

Environmental Impact:

1. **Energy Efficiency:** Automation optimizes resource usage, leading to reduced energy consumption.

2. **Sustainability:** AI aids in analyzing data to identify eco-friendly practices and optimize resource allocation.

Conclusion: "AI and Automation: Streamlining Business for Maximum Gain" encapsulates the powerful convergence of technological advancements that reshape the business landscape. By harnessing AI's cognitive capabilities and automation's efficiency, businesses can achieve unprecedented levels of operational excellence, resource optimization, and customer satisfaction. This journey into AI and automation underscores their transformative potential, paving the way for innovation, job creation, and sustainable growth while navigating ethical considerations and addressing challenges. As businesses leverage the full spectrum of AI and automation, they unlock a new era of efficiency, productivity, and competitive advantage that propels them towards maximum gain in an increasingly interconnected and data-driven world.

CHAPTER 31: CRISIS AS CATALYST: TURNING CHALLENGES INTO OPPORTUNITIES

Introduction: In the tapestry of human history, crises have often been pivotal moments that spurred transformation and progress. "Crisis as Catalyst: Turning Challenges into Opportunities" delves into the remarkable phenomenon where adversity, instead of paralyzing, becomes a driving force for innovation, growth, and positive change. This exploration unravels the intricate ways in which individuals, organizations, and societies navigate through crises, uncovering the mechanisms that enable transformation, the psychology of resilience, the impact on various sectors, and the profound potential to emerge stronger and more adaptable.

Understanding Crisis as a Catalyst:

1. **Redefining Challenges:** A crisis reframes challenges as opportunities for growth, learning, and transformation.

2. **Innovation in Adversity:** Necessity drives innovation as individuals and organizations find new ways to overcome obstacles.

The Psychology of Resilience:

1. **Adaptive Coping:** Resilience allows individuals to adapt and cope effectively with adversity.

2. **Post-Traumatic Growth:** Some individuals experience personal growth and positive change after overcoming trauma.

Transformation Through Crisis:

1. **Economic Transformations:** Crises often reshape economies, prompting the emergence of new industries and markets.

2. **Social Innovations:** Crisis catalyzes social initiatives addressing inequality, health disparities, and community well-being.

Business and Entrepreneurial Resilience:

1. **Agile Business Models:** Organizations pivot to meet changing demands, harnessing new opportunities.

2. **Entrepreneurial Adaptation:** Crisis prompts entrepreneurs to identify unmet needs and create innovative solutions.

Education and Workforce Evolution:

1. **Remote Learning Revolution:** Crises accelerate the adoption of online education and digital skill development.

2. **New Work Paradigms:** Remote work becomes a norm, reshaping work-life balance and employment models.

Crisis-Driven Technological Leaps:

1. **Technological Adoption:** Crises drive the rapid adoption of technologies for remote communication, collaboration, and digital transformation.

2. **Healthcare Innovations:** Medical crises spur innovations in telemedicine, remote patient monitoring, and healthcare delivery.

Global Cooperation and Diplomacy:

1. **Collaborative Solutions:** Crises necessitate global cooperation to address shared challenges such as climate change and pandemics.

2. **Diplomatic Innovation:** Diplomacy adapts to crisis situations, fostering international partnerships for recovery.

The Power of Collective Action:

1. **Community Support:** Crises foster community

solidarity, as individuals unite to support one another.

2. **Activism and Advocacy:** Adversity sparks social and political movements that drive systemic change.

Overcoming Obstacles and Learning from Failure:

1. **Grit and Determination:** Facing adversity cultivates resilience, grit, and the capacity to persist in the face of challenges.

2. **Learning from Failure:** Crises expose vulnerabilities, prompting reflection and adaptation to prevent future setbacks.

Sustainable Growth and Adaptation:

1. **Rebuilding Better:** Post-crisis recovery focuses on building more sustainable, resilient, and equitable systems.

2. **Continuous Adaptation:** The ability to adapt remains crucial, ensuring readiness for future challenges.

Conclusion: "Crisis as Catalyst: Turning Challenges into Opportunities" celebrates the remarkable human capacity to transform adversity into catalysts for growth, innovation, and positive change. Through resilience, determination, and a willingness to adapt, individuals, organizations, and societies harness crises to drive progress in diverse sectors, from business and education to technology and diplomacy. This journey into the transformative power of crises underscores the potential for profound impact, adaptation, and resilience, guiding humanity to emerge from challenges not only stronger but also better equipped to navigate the uncertainties of an ever-evolving world.

CHAPTER 32: THE EVOLUTION OF LEADERSHIP: BUILDING AND LEADING EMPIRES

Introduction: Throughout history, leaders have played a pivotal role in shaping empires and civilizations, guiding societies through challenges, and driving monumental change. "The Evolution of Leadership: Building and Leading Empires" delves into the multifaceted journey of leaders who have risen to power, conquered vast territories, and left an indelible mark on history. This exploration unravels the characteristics, strategies, and principles that defined these leaders, their influence on the growth of empires, and the lessons they offer for modern leadership in an ever-changing world.

The Foundations of Leadership:

1. **Leadership Traits:** Effective leaders possess traits such as vision, charisma, decisiveness, and adaptability.

2. **Leadership Styles:** Different leaders adopt styles ranging from autocratic to transformational, adapting to their context.

Ancient Empires and Founding Leaders:

1. **Alexander the Great:** His visionary conquests spread Hellenistic culture across vast territories.

2. **Julius Caesar:** A military and political genius who played a crucial role in transforming the Roman Republic into the Roman Empire.

Empires of the Middle Ages and Renaissance:

1. **Charlemagne:** United much of Western Europe and laid the foundations for the Holy Roman Empire.

2. **Genghis Khan:** His unparalleled strategic prowess led

to the creation of the largest contiguous land empire in history.

Modern Empires and Industrial Revolution:

1. **Napoleon Bonaparte:** His military genius and vision reshaped Europe, leaving a lasting impact on modern governance.

2. **Queen Victoria:** Symbolizing the British Empire's peak, her reign coincided with significant technological and societal changes.

Leadership Lessons from Empires:

1. **Strategic Vision:** Empirical leaders demonstrated far-reaching vision and ambition for their empires.

2. **Adaptability:** Successful leaders adapted to changing circumstances and seized opportunities for expansion.

The Role of Communication and Influence:

1. **Charismatic Authority:** Many empire builders had a magnetic charisma that inspired loyalty and motivated followers.

2. **Cultural Diplomacy:** Leaders skillfully navigated cultural differences, forging alliances through diplomacy.

Challenges of Leadership and Legacy:

1. **Maintaining Control:** Balancing centralized power with regional autonomy was a challenge for many empires.

2. **Legacy and Impact:** The legacy of empire builders often extends beyond their lifetimes, shaping culture, politics, and international relations.

Modern Leadership in a Globalized World:

1. **Globalization and Technology:** Leaders today navigate a fast-paced, interconnected world, leveraging technology and diplomacy.

2. **Ethical Leadership:** The emphasis on ethics and social responsibility influences modern leadership dynamics.

Leadership in Uncertain Times:

1. **Crisis Management:** Leaders must navigate crises effectively, making tough decisions for the greater good.

2. **Inclusive Leadership:** Embracing diversity and fostering inclusivity are central to modern leadership.

Building and Leading Empires in the 21st Century:

1. **Economic Empires:** Modern leaders create global economic influence through multinational corporations and digital platforms.

2. **Soft Power and Diplomacy:** Soft power, cultural exchange, and diplomacy play a pivotal role in modern empire building.

Conclusion: "The Evolution of Leadership: Building and Leading Empires" unveils the extraordinary journeys of leaders who shaped empires across epochs, offering timeless insights for contemporary leadership. The legacy of these leaders resonates through history, their triumphs and challenges providing a rich tapestry of lessons in vision, adaptation, communication, and ethical governance. As the world continues to evolve, modern leaders draw inspiration from the strategies of empire builders, adapting them to navigate the complexities of a globalized, interconnected world, where the essence of leadership remains rooted in the ability to inspire, adapt, and shape the course of history.

CHAPTER 33: CULTURAL CAPITAL: UNDERSTANDING DIVERSE MARKET DEMANDS

Introduction: In a globalized world characterized by diverse cultures, understanding and harnessing cultural capital has become imperative for businesses seeking to thrive in various markets. "Cultural Capital: Understanding Diverse Market Demands" delves into the intricate landscape where cultural nuances, values, traditions, and preferences shape consumer behavior, business strategies, and market dynamics. This exploration unravels the multifaceted dimensions of cultural capital, encompassing cross-cultural communication, localization, cultural intelligence, inclusivity, and the profound impact of cultural understanding on market success and sustainable growth.

Cultural Capital Defined:

1. **Cultural Intelligence:** The ability to comprehend and adapt to cultural differences, enabling effective cross-cultural interactions.

2. **Cultural Capital:** The wealth of knowledge and understanding accumulated by individuals and organizations about different cultures.

Cultural Dynamics in Consumer Behavior:

1. **Cultural Norms and Values:** Consumer preferences are influenced by cultural norms, values, and societal expectations.

2. **Cultural Significance:** Products often hold cultural significance, influencing their desirability and relevance.

Cultural Sensitivity and Inclusivity:

1. **Respectful Marketing:** Businesses must navigate cultural sensitivities to avoid cultural appropriation or insensitivity.

2. **Inclusive Marketing:** Tailoring strategies to embrace diverse cultures fosters inclusivity and broadens customer bases.

Cross-Cultural Communication:

1. **Language and Communication:** Language barriers impact communication effectiveness, requiring translation and localization.

2. **Nonverbal Communication:** Nonverbal cues, gestures, and body language vary across cultures and require understanding.

Localization and Customization:

1. **Localization Strategy:** Adapting products, services, and marketing messages to align with local cultures and preferences.

2. **Customization:** Allowing customers to personalize products to suit cultural or individual preferences.

Global Brands and Local Adaptation:

1. **Global Consistency:** Balancing consistency across global branding with adaptations for local tastes.

2. **Glocalization:** Merging global and local strategies to create offerings that resonate universally while addressing local needs.

Cultural Intelligence and Business Success:

1. **Cultural Competency:** Businesses with high cultural intelligence are better equipped to navigate global markets.

2. **Negotiation and Relationship Building:** Cultural understanding enhances negotiation and relationship-

building efforts.

Challenges of Cultural Capital:

1. **Stereotyping and Assumptions:** Incorrect assumptions about cultural preferences can lead to marketing failures.

2. **Cultural Bias:** Unconscious bias can hinder effective cross-cultural communication and decision-making.

Cultural Capital in Talent Management:

1. **Diverse Workforce:** Cultural intelligence fosters a diverse and inclusive work environment.

2. **Global Teams:** Effectively managing teams across cultures requires understanding and accommodating differences.

Technological and Globalization Impact:

1. **E-Commerce and Global Markets:** Technology enables businesses to reach diverse markets, necessitating cultural understanding.

2. **Digital Localization:** Websites, apps, and content must be localized to resonate with users from different cultures.

Cultural Capital and Innovation:

1. **Cultural Diversity and Creativity:** Exposure to diverse cultures fuels innovation and creative problem-solving.

2. **Adopting Best Practices:** Learning from different cultural approaches to business and problem-solving enhances strategic thinking.

Conclusion: "Cultural Capital: Understanding Diverse Market Demands" underscores the pivotal role of cultural understanding in navigating global markets successfully. By harnessing cultural intelligence, businesses can transcend barriers, foster inclusivity, and tailor strategies that resonate with diverse consumer bases.

This journey through the realm of cultural capital emphasizes the fusion of cultural empathy, respect, and adaptability, guiding businesses to not only meet market demands but also create meaningful connections and sustainable growth in an ever-evolving world enriched by its cultural diversity.

CHAPTER 34: REIMAGINING RETIREMENT: FINANCIAL FREEDOM IN LATER LIFE

Introduction: The concept of retirement is undergoing a transformative shift as individuals seek to redefine their later years as a period of financial freedom, purpose, and fulfillment. "Reimagining Retirement: Financial Freedom in Later Life" delves into the evolving landscape of retirement, exploring strategies for achieving financial security, creating meaningful lifestyles, and finding purpose beyond traditional retirement age. This exploration uncovers the multidimensional facets of reimagined retirement, including financial planning, health and wellness, lifelong learning, entrepreneurship, and the profound potential for a vibrant and fulfilling later life.

Changing Paradigms of Retirement:

1. **Retirement Redefined:** Retirement is no longer just about leisure; it's a phase for personal growth and pursuing passions.

2. **Extended Life Expectancy:** Longer lifespans challenge traditional retirement models, demanding new approaches.

Financial Planning for a Secure Future:

1. **Early Planning:** Strategic financial planning during one's career sets the stage for a comfortable retirement.

2. **Diversified Investments:** A well-balanced investment portfolio helps sustain income streams during retirement.

Health and Wellness for Longevity:

1. **Holistic Wellbeing:** Prioritizing physical, mental, and emotional health contributes to a more active

retirement.

2. **Preventive Care:** Taking proactive health measures enhances quality of life and reduces healthcare expenses.

Lifelong Learning and Skill Development:

1. **Continuous Learning:** Engaging in lifelong learning pursuits keeps the mind active and sharp.

2. **New Ventures:** Acquiring new skills can lead to second careers, consulting roles, or entrepreneurship.

Entrepreneurship and Post-Retirement Ventures:

1. **Encore Careers:** Entrepreneurial ventures in retirement offer income and purpose while following passions.

2. **Creative Pursuits:** Turning hobbies into income-generating activities adds fulfillment to the retirement journey.

Community Engagement and Social Networks:

1. **Social Capital:** Building and maintaining strong social connections enhances emotional wellbeing.

2. **Volunteering and Mentorship:** Engaging in community activities and mentoring fosters a sense of purpose.

Challenges of Reimagined Retirement:

1. **Financial Risks:** Longevity risk and unexpected expenses challenge retirement planning.

2. **Identity Shift:** Transitioning from a career-focused identity to a retiree can pose psychological challenges.

Retirement Abroad and International Living:

1. **Global Living:** Some retirees opt for lower-cost countries that offer a higher quality of life.

2. **Healthcare Considerations:** Access to quality healthcare is a vital factor when considering retiring abroad.

Creating a Legacy and Giving Back:

1. **Generational Wealth:** Planning for intergenerational wealth transfer ensures a lasting impact on family.

2. **Philanthropy:** Giving back through charitable endeavors supports causes close to one's heart.

Technological Empowerment in Retirement:

1. **Digital Literacy:** Embracing technology opens doors to online work, remote learning, and social connections.

2. **Digital Entrepreneurship:** Online platforms enable retirees to market skills, products, or services globally.

Conclusion: "Reimagining Retirement: Financial Freedom in Later Life" showcases the exciting paradigm shift from traditional retirement to a stage of life brimming with possibilities. By embracing financial planning, health and wellness, ongoing learning, entrepreneurship, and community engagement, individuals can forge a path to a retirement characterized by vibrancy, purpose, and continued personal growth. This journey into the reimagined retirement underscores the importance of adapting to changing times, seizing opportunities, and nurturing holistic well-being, ultimately unlocking a life phase that transcends mere relaxation to become a period of fulfillment, contribution, and lasting significance.

CHAPTER 35: THE FUTURE OF WORK: THRIVING IN THE GIG ECONOMY

Introduction: The global workforce is undergoing a paradigm shift as the traditional 9-to-5 model gives way to the dynamic and flexible landscape of the gig economy. "The Future of Work: Thriving in the Gig Economy" delves into the transformative nature of work, exploring the intricacies of gig employment, its impact on career trajectories, economic systems, and the strategies individuals can employ to excel and find fulfillment in this evolving landscape. This exploration uncovers the multifaceted dimensions of the gig economy, from its characteristics and challenges to its potential for innovation, work-life balance, and reshaping the very nature of work.

Understanding the Gig Economy:

1. **Definition of Gig Economy:** The gig economy comprises temporary, freelance, and project-based work, often facilitated by digital platforms.

2. **Characteristics:** Flexibility, independence, and the ability to work on diverse projects are hallmarks of the gig economy.

Benefits and Challenges of Gig Work:

1. **Flexibility:** Gig work allows individuals to design their own schedules and manage work-life balance.

2. **Income Variability:** Irregular income and lack of benefits can pose financial challenges for gig workers.

Entrepreneurship and Skill Monetization:

1. **Personal Branding:** Gig workers market their skills and build personal brands to attract clients.

2. **Portfolio Careers:** Many gig workers combine multiple

sources of income for stability and variety.

Adapting to Uncertainty:

1. **Financial Planning:** Gig workers need robust financial plans to navigate income fluctuations.

2. **Professional Development:** Continuous skill development ensures relevance in a rapidly changing job landscape.

The Role of Digital Platforms:

1. **Platform Diversity:** Platforms like Uber, Upwork, and Airbnb offer opportunities across industries.

2. **Digital Skills:** Navigating the gig economy requires proficiency in digital tools and online communication.

Gig Economy and Work-Life Balance:

1. **Customized Schedules:** Gig workers can tailor their work hours to suit personal preferences and commitments.

2. **Burnout Risk:** Balancing multiple projects can lead to burnout without careful time management.

Impact on Traditional Employment:

1. **Shifting Employer-Employee Dynamics:** Employers increasingly hire gig workers for specific projects, impacting traditional employment models.

2. **Economic Implications:** The gig economy challenges traditional social safety nets and benefits systems.

Innovation and Creativity:

1. **Innovation Ecosystem:** Gig work fosters creativity, allowing individuals to explore diverse projects and industries.

2. **Entrepreneurial Mindset:** Gig workers often adopt an entrepreneurial mindset, contributing to innovation.

Legal and Ethical Considerations:

1. **Worker Classification:** Determining whether gig workers are contractors or employees has legal and economic implications.

2. **Fair Compensation:** Ensuring fair pay and protection for gig workers is an ongoing ethical debate.

Remote Work and Gig Opportunities:

1. **Global Reach:** Remote work allows gig workers to collaborate with clients and teams worldwide.

2. **Cultural Competence:** Remote gigs require cultural sensitivity to communicate effectively across borders.

Future of Work in the Gig Economy:

1. **Evolving Job Structures:** Traditional job roles are becoming more fluid, embracing gig-like characteristics.

2. **Hybrid Models:** Some organizations adopt hybrid employment models, combining full-time and gig workers.

Conclusion: "The Future of Work: Thriving in the Gig Economy" underscores the transformative nature of work, where adaptability, innovation, and skill diversification are paramount. By embracing the gig economy, individuals can craft flexible and fulfilling careers, leveraging technology, personal branding, and continuous learning. This journey into the gig economy realm highlights the need for resilience, financial planning, and an entrepreneurial mindset to navigate its challenges and unlock its opportunities. Ultimately, the gig economy stands as a beacon of change, shaping not only the nature of work but also the very fabric of modern employment, offering a platform for individuals to define their own paths and find success on their own terms.

CHAPTER 36: MASTERING MONEY: STRATEGIES FOR WEALTH ACCUMULATION

Introduction: In an intricate financial landscape, mastering money becomes essential for securing financial stability, achieving goals, and building wealth. "Mastering Money: Strategies for Wealth Accumulation" delves into the multifaceted realm of financial management, exploring the strategies, principles, and practices that empower individuals to accumulate wealth, make informed decisions, and attain long-term financial security. This exploration uncovers the diverse dimensions of financial mastery, encompassing budgeting, saving, investing, debt management, risk mitigation, and the profound potential for achieving financial freedom and prosperity.

Foundations of Financial Mastery:

1. **Financial Literacy:** Understanding financial concepts, terminology, and tools is fundamental to mastering money.

2. **Mindset Shift:** Adopting a growth mindset and cultivating a positive relationship with money are key.

Budgeting and Expense Management:

1. **Creating a Budget:** Crafting a comprehensive budget help allocate funds wisely and control spending.

2. **Expense Tracking:** Monitoring expenses provides insight into financial habits and identifies areas for improvement.

Strategies for Saving and Emergency Funds:

1. **Automated Savings:** Setting up automated transfers to savings accounts ensures consistent saving.

2. **Emergency Funds:** Building a safety net for unexpected expenses is a cornerstone of financial security.

Investment Principles for Wealth Accumulation:

1. **Diversification:** Spreading investments across different asset classes reduces risk and enhances returns.

2. **Compounding:** Harnessing the power of compounding interest accelerates wealth accumulation over time.

Risk Management and Insurance:

1. **Insurance Coverage:** Adequate insurance safeguards against unexpected financial setbacks.

2. **Asset Protection:** Establishing legal and financial structures safeguards assets from potential risks.

Debt Management and Financial Leverage:

1. **Good vs. Bad Debt:** Differentiating between productive debt (e.g., education, real estate) and detrimental debt (e.g., high-interest consumer debt).

2. **Leveraging Assets:** Using debt strategically to invest in appreciating assets can amplify wealth growth.

Real Estate and Alternative Investments:

1. **Real Estate:** Property ownership and investment diversify wealth and provide rental income potential.

2. **Alternative Investments:** Exploring investments beyond traditional stocks and bonds for portfolio diversification.

Retirement Planning and Long-Term Goals:

1. **Retirement Accounts:** Contributing to retirement accounts, such as 401(k)s and IRAs, ensures long-term financial security.

2. **Goal Setting:** Defining specific financial goals and creating plans to achieve them is integral.

Tax Optimization Strategies:

1. **Tax-Efficient Investing:** Maximizing tax efficiency in investments can significantly impact overall returns.

2. **Tax Planning:** Employing tax strategies to minimize liability and retain more income.

Estate Planning and Generational Wealth:

1. **Wills and Trusts:** Crafting an estate plan ensures the seamless transfer of wealth to beneficiaries.

2. **Legacy and Philanthropy:** Planning for charitable giving and passing down values to future generations.

Financial Education and Continuous Learning:

1. **Staying Informed:** Keeping up with financial news, trends, and investment opportunities enhances decision-making.

2. **Professional Guidance:** Consulting financial advisors and experts adds depth to financial strategies.

Conclusion: "Mastering Money: Strategies for Wealth Accumulation" underscores the transformative power of financial education and prudent decision-making in securing long-term financial prosperity. By employing strategies that encompass budgeting, saving, investing, risk management, and long-term planning, individuals can navigate the complexities of wealth accumulation and achieve financial freedom. This journey through the world of financial mastery underscores the importance of discipline, adaptability, and informed choices in shaping a future of financial security, enabling individuals to unlock the potential for growth, wealth, and the pursuit of life's most meaningful goals.

CHAPTER 37: LEGAL STRATEGIES FOR ASSET PROTECTION AND GROWTH

Introduction: In an intricate financial landscape, safeguarding assets and nurturing their growth is paramount for individuals and businesses alike. "Legal Strategies for Asset Protection and Growth" delves into the multifaceted realm of legal tactics and frameworks that empower individuals and businesses to shield their assets from risks while fostering sustainable wealth accumulation. This exploration uncovers the intricate dimensions of asset protection, encompassing legal structures, risk mitigation, estate planning, business entities, and the profound potential to achieve both security and growth through strategic legal measures.

Understanding Asset Protection:

1. **Asset Vulnerabilities:** Assets are vulnerable to risks such as lawsuits, creditor claims, and economic downturns.

2. **Legal Safeguards:** Utilizing legal strategies helps mitigate threats and protect assets from potential loss.

Legal Structures for Asset Protection:

1. **Limited Liability Companies (LLCs):** LLCs shield personal assets from business liabilities, preserving personal wealth.

2. **Family Limited Partnerships (FLPs):** FLPs facilitate wealth transfer and provide protection against creditor claims.

Estate Planning and Wealth Preservation:

1. **Wills and Trusts:** Creating wills and trusts ensures orderly asset distribution and minimizes estate taxes.

2. **Generation-Skipping Trusts:** These trusts preserve assets for future generations while minimizing tax burdens.

Business Entities and Asset Segregation:

1. **Corporations:** Corporations provide liability protection by separating business assets from personal assets.

2. **Limited Partnerships (LPs):** LPs offer asset protection for limited partners while enabling active business management.

Domestic and Offshore Trusts:

1. **Domestic Asset Protection Trusts (DAPTs):** Some states offer DAPTs, shielding assets from creditors.

2. **Offshore Trusts:** Offshore trusts provide legal insulation from domestic legal actions.

Insurance and Risk Management:

1. **Umbrella Insurance:** Umbrella policies provide an additional layer of liability protection beyond standard coverage.

2. **Professional Liability Insurance:** Professionals can safeguard assets from lawsuits through specialized coverage.

Bankruptcy Protection and Exemptions:

1. **Homestead Exemptions:** These exemptions protect home equity from creditors during bankruptcy proceedings.

2. **Retirement Accounts:** Retirement accounts are often exempt from bankruptcy claims, safeguarding retirement savings.

Cohabitation and Premarital Agreements:

1. **Cohabitation Agreements:** Unmarried couples can create agreements to define property rights and

obligations.

2. **Prenuptial Agreements:** Prenups outline asset division and financial responsibilities in the event of divorce.

International Asset Protection:

1. **Foreign Holding Structures:** Utilizing foreign entities can provide legal insulation from domestic claims.

2. **Offshore Banking:** Offshore accounts offer privacy and protection from potential domestic disputes.

Intellectual Property Protection:

1. **Trademarks and Patents:** Protecting intellectual property rights prevents unauthorized use and potential infringement claims.

2. **Licensing Agreements:** Licensing IP to others can generate income while safeguarding the asset.

Legal Compliance and Ethical Considerations:

1. **Fraudulent Conveyance Laws:** Transferring assets to evade creditors can result in legal consequences.

2. **Ethical Obligations:** Asset protection measures must align with ethical and legal standards.

Conclusion: "Legal Strategies for Asset Protection and Growth" underscores the critical importance of employing robust legal tactics to secure assets while fostering growth and prosperity. By harnessing legal structures, estate planning, business entities, and insurance, individuals and businesses can navigate risks, protect their assets, and nurture long-term wealth growth. This journey through the realm of asset protection and growth emphasizes the synergy between legal insight, strategic planning, and ethical considerations in shaping a future marked by security, opportunity, and sustainable financial success.

CHAPTER 38: THE PSYCHOLOGY OF NEGOTIATION: SEALING LUCRATIVE DEALS

Introduction: Negotiation is an art form that transcends business transactions; it's a complex interplay of psychology, strategy, and communication that shapes the outcomes of interactions. "The Psychology of Negotiation: Sealing Lucrative Deals" delves into the intricate world of negotiation, exploring the psychological underpinnings that drive successful deal-making. This exploration uncovers the multifaceted dimensions of negotiation psychology, from understanding cognitive biases to building rapport, strategic communication, and the profound potential to achieve mutually beneficial outcomes and lasting relationships.

Understanding Negotiation Psychology:

1. **Cognitive Biases:** Acknowledging cognitive biases helps negotiators anticipate and counteract biased decision-making.

2. **Emotional Intelligence:** Recognizing emotions and responding empathetically enhances negotiation outcomes.

Building Rapport and Trust:

1. **Establishing Connection:** Creating rapport establishes a foundation of trust that fosters effective communication.

2. **Active Listening:** Attentive listening shows respect, facilitates understanding, and builds rapport.

Persuasion and Influence:

1. **Reciprocity:** Offering concessions initiates a cycle of reciprocation, increasing the likelihood of agreement.

2. **Social Proof:** Demonstrating how others have benefited reinforces the value of the proposed deal.

Anchoring and Framing:

1. **Anchoring Effect:** Setting an initial offer influences subsequent negotiation point.
2. **Framing:** Presenting information in different ways shapes perceptions and influences decisions.

Win-Win Mindset:

1. **Collaborative Negotiation:** Focusing on mutual gains cultivates long-term relationships and positive outcomes.
2. **Negotiation Strategies:** Win-win outcomes often involve creative problem-solving and value-adding propositions.

Power Dynamics and BATNA:

1. **Power Imbalance:** Understanding power dynamics helps negotiators leverage strengths and mitigate weaknesses.
2. **Best Alternative to a Negotiated Agreement (BATNA):** Knowing one's BATNA sets a negotiation benchmark.

Negotiation Styles and Cultural Sensitivity:

1. **Competitive vs. Collaborative:** Different negotiation styles align with diverse goals and scenarios.
2. **Cultural Adaptability:** Cultural nuances influence negotiation dynamics; sensitivity is crucial.

Negotiation Strategies:

1. **Distributive Negotiation:** Maximizing gains in single-issue, zero-sum negotiations requires careful strategy.
2. **Integrative Negotiation:** Collaborative problem-solving identifies common interests and expands the value pie.

Managing Conflict and Difficult People:

1. **Conflict Resolution:** Addressing conflicts openly and finding common ground defuses tensions.

2. **Difficult Personalities:** Strategies for negotiating with difficult individuals include remaining composed and empathetic.

Negotiation Ethics:

1. **Integrity and Honesty:** Ethical negotiations prioritize truthfulness and transparency.

2. **Long-Term Relationships:** Ethical conduct builds trust for future interactions.

Strategic Communication:

1. **Questioning Techniques:** Effective questioning uncovers needs and priorities, facilitating targeted proposals.

2. **Effective Persuasion:** Communicating benefits that align with the other party's interests drives agreement.

Conclusion: "The Psychology of Negotiation: Sealing Lucrative Deals" underscores the intricate interplay of psychology, strategy, and communication in successful negotiations. By understanding cognitive biases, building rapport, employing persuasive tactics, and embracing a win-win mindset, negotiators can navigate complex negotiations with finesse. This journey through the world of negotiation psychology emphasizes the art of empathy, strategic thinking, and ethical conduct in shaping agreements that not only fulfill short-term objectives but also foster long-term relationships built on trust, collaboration, and mutual benefit.

CHAPTER 39: LEGACY BUILDING: PASSING ON WEALTH AND WISDOM

Introduction: Legacy building is an intricate process that transcends mere financial inheritance; it's about shaping a narrative of impact, values, and wisdom that endures beyond one's lifetime. "Legacy Building: Passing On Wealth and Wisdom" delves into the multifaceted journey of creating a meaningful legacy, exploring the harmonious convergence of financial planning, values, family dynamics, philanthropy, and the profound potential to shape a lasting heritage that transcends generations. This exploration uncovers the intricate dimensions of legacy building, from financial strategies to imparting wisdom, preserving family harmony, and the transformative power of contributing to the greater good.

Defining Legacy Building:

1. **Beyond Wealth:** Legacy encompasses not just financial assets, but also values, principles, and stories.

2. **Generational Impact:** A well-crafted legacy influences future generations' behavior, aspirations, and purpose.

Financial Planning for Legacy:

1. **Estate Planning:** Crafting wills, trusts, and estate documents ensures a smooth wealth transfer.

2. **Generational Wealth Transfer:** Structuring inheritances responsibly supports financial literacy and long-term prosperity.

Values and Family Unity:

1. **Family Mission Statements:** Defining shared values and goals fosters family unity and collaboration.

2. **Interpersonal Communication:** Open dialogue

promotes understanding, reducing conflicts in generational transitions.

Wisdom Transmission:

1. **Life Lessons:** Sharing personal experiences imparts wisdom that guides future generations.

2. **Mentorship:** Actively mentoring younger family members nurtures growth and character development.

Philanthropy and Social Impact:

1. **Charitable Giving:** Incorporating philanthropy into a legacy instills values of empathy and community contribution.

2. **Creating Change:** Leaving a positive impact through charitable work establishes a legacy of change.

Family Business Succession:

1. **Transition Planning:** Succession planning ensures the seamless continuation of family businesses.

2. **Balancing Interests:** Addressing varying aspirations and skills of family members is key for a successful transition.

Education and Continuous Learning:

1. **Education Funds:** Establishing funds for education nurtures knowledge transfer across generations.

2. **Lifelong Learning:** Encouraging a culture of continuous learning keeps family members adaptable and engaged.

Preserving Cultural Heritage:

1. **Cultural Traditions:** Passing down cultural practices maintains a connection to ancestral roots.

2. **Language and Identity:** Upholding native languages preserves cultural heritage and strengthens family bonds.

Emotional Intelligence and Conflict Resolution:

1. **Conflict Management:** Building emotional intelligence helps resolve conflicts constructively.

2. **Family Governance:** Developing governance structures facilitates decision-making and conflict resolution.

Longevity and Adaptive Planning:

1. **Adapting to Change:** Dynamic legacy planning evolves with changing family dynamics and external factors.

2. **Multigenerational Impact:** A well-designed legacy accommodates the aspirations of multiple generations.

Conclusion: "Legacy Building: Passing On Wealth and Wisdom" underscores the profound impact of creating a legacy that resonates far beyond material wealth. By merging financial strategies, values, wisdom, philanthropy, and fostering harmonious family dynamics, individuals can shape a legacy that transcends generations, perpetuates their values, and creates a lasting impact on society. This journey through the realm of legacy building emphasizes the delicate balance between wealth preservation and wisdom transmission, guiding families to craft a narrative of success, unity, and purpose that echoes through time, enriching lives, and leaving an indelible imprint on the world.

CHAPTER 40: THE CONTINUED JOURNEY: SUSTAINING PROSPERITY IN FLUX

Introduction: The pursuit of prosperity is an ongoing journey marked by continuous evolution and adaptation. "The Continued Journey: Sustaining Prosperity in Flux" delves into the intricate nature of maintaining success and prosperity amidst a dynamic and ever-changing landscape. This exploration unravels the multifaceted dimensions of sustaining prosperity, encompassing resilience, innovation, strategic planning, adaptability, and the profound potential to endure through challenges while achieving consistent growth and fulfillment.

Understanding Sustaining Prosperity:

1. **Dynamic Environment:** Prosperity exists in a constantly changing environment, demanding ongoing adjustments.

2. **Holistic Approach:** Sustaining prosperity involves balance across financial, personal, and professional aspects.

Resilience in the Face of Challenges:

1. **Adversity and Growth:** Challenges stimulate growth and innovation, fostering long-term prosperity.

2. **Crisis Management:** Resilience in times of crisis ensures continuity and opportunity for growth.

Innovation and Evolution:

1. **Continuous Innovation:** Adapting and evolving products, services, and strategies keeps businesses relevant.

2. **Disruptive Thinking:** Embracing disruptive

technologies and ideas drives innovation.

Strategic Planning for Longevity:

1. **Vision and Mission:** Defining a clear vision and mission guides decision-making and strategic direction.

2. **Scenario Planning:** Identifying potential future scenarios allows proactive preparation.

Adaptability and Flexibility:

1. **Agile Operations:** Businesses that can pivot quickly are better positioned to seize new opportunities.

2. **Change Management:** Navigating change with flexibility minimizes disruption and maximizes growth.

Human Capital and Organizational Growth:

1. **Talent Development:** Nurturing employee skills and potential drives organizational success.

2. **Leadership Succession:** Developing a pipeline of capable leaders ensures continuity.

Embracing Technological Advancements:

1. **Digital Transformation:** Integrating technology optimizes operations and enhances customer experience.

2. **Automation and Efficiency:** Adopting automation streamlines processes and reduces inefficiencies.

Environmental Sustainability:

1. **Corporate Responsibility:** Embracing sustainable practices demonstrates commitment to future generations.

2. **Economic Impact:** Sustainable practices can lead to cost savings and increased customer loyalty.

Building Resilient Financial Foundations:

1. **Diversification:** Spreading investments minimizes risk

and supports long-term growth.

2. **Emergency Funds:** Maintaining liquidity provides a safety net during economic downturns.

Balancing Short-Term Goals with Long-Term Vision:

1. **Strategic Patience:** Balancing immediate goals with long-term objectives ensures sustained success.

2. **Consistent Progress:** Gradual, consistent progress often yields more sustainable results.

Cultural Adaptation and Market Shifts:

1. **Global Awareness:** Understanding diverse cultures and markets fosters adaptability and growth.

2. **Market Trend Anticipation:** Monitoring and adapting to changing consumer preferences secures market relevance.

Conclusion: "The Continued Journey: Sustaining Prosperity in Flux" underscores the enduring nature of prosperity and the strategies that enable its continuity. By embracing resilience, innovation, strategic planning, and adaptability, individuals and organizations can navigate the ever-changing landscape and sustain success even amidst challenges. This journey through the realm of sustaining prosperity emphasizes the delicate balance between stability and growth, guiding individuals and businesses to not only weather uncertainties but also flourish, achieve meaningful impact, and leave a lasting legacy of resilience and prosperity for generations to come.

EPILOGUE

As we close the final chapter of "The Modern Millionaire Matrix: Blueprint for 21st Century Wealth," we find ourselves at the crossroads of inspiration and action, armed with insights that transcend the pages of this book. This journey has been one of exploration, discovery, and empowerment—an odyssey into the heart of contemporary wealth creation and the ever-evolving landscape of the 21st century.

The matrix we've navigated together is not just a theoretical construct; it's a dynamic canvas that invites you to apply the principles, strategies, and mindsets to your own unique path toward prosperity. Throughout these pages, we've delved into the mindset shift from scarcity to abundance, embraced the power of disruptive innovation, harnessed technology, seized investment opportunities, and ventured into the realms of social capital and personal branding.

The modern millionaire's journey is an intricate dance between traditional wisdom and innovative thinking. It's about mastering the art of adaptability in the face of change, recognizing that wealth isn't solely about monetary abundance but also encompasses knowledge, impact, and a legacy that transcends generations. It's the pursuit of a wealth that resonates with the values of the digital age—a wealth that thrives on collaboration, innovation, and the boundless possibilities of the global marketplace.

As you reflect on the insights you've gained, remember that this is just the beginning. The blueprint laid out before you are a living document—a canvas awaiting your brushstrokes of innovation, resilience, and determination. The modern millionaire's matrix evolves with the times, and your journey will be marked by the choices you make, the strategies you implement, and the impact you create.

Whether you're an entrepreneur carving out your niche in the digital landscape, an investor seeking unconventional opportunities, or a visionary leader shaping the future, the principles unveiled in this book are your allies. They are the foundation upon which you can build your empire of innovation, your legacy of impact, and your pathway to prosperity.

The journey toward modern wealth is not without its challenges and uncertainties, but it's also brimming with potential, growth, and fulfillment. As you step forward, armed with the wisdom gleaned from these pages, remember that you possess the tools to adapt, thrive, and shape a future that aligns with the ever-changing currents of our dynamic world.

So, as you embark on your own continued journey, may you channel the mindset of abundance, embrace the spirit of innovation, and navigate the complexities of the 21st century with courage and confidence. The matrix is yours to explore, refine, and reshape, and the legacy you build will be a testament to your commitment to modern prosperity—a prosperity that not only enriches your life but also contributes to the greater tapestry of progress, innovation, and success.

The End.

www.ingramcontent.com/pod-product-compliance
Lightning Source LLC
Chambersburg PA
CBHW072301290526
45794CB00002B/521